THE WESTERN FRONTIER LIBRARY

(For complete list, see page 251)

A Lady's Life
in the Rocky Mountains

A Lady's Life in the Rocky Mountains

by Isabella L. Bird

With an introduction by Daniel J. Boorstin

*

NORMAN : UNIVERSITY OF OKLAHOMA PRESS

LIBRARY OF CONGRESS CATALOG CARD NUMBER: 60–8748

New edition copyright 1960 by the University of Oklahoma Press, Publishing Division of the University. Composed and printed at Norman, Oklahoma, U.S.A., by the University of Oklahoma Press. First printing, April, 1960; second printing, October, 1962; third printing, January, 1965; fourth printing, November, 1966; fifth printing, April, 1969.

To My Sister,
to whom
these letters were originally written,
they are now
affectionately dedicated.

Contents

✳

✲⊚✦✲⊚✦✲⊚✦✲⊚✦✲⊚✦✲⊚✦✲⊚✦✲⊚✦✲⊚✦✲⊚✦✲⊚

Illustrations

✳

✦✳↩✤✦✳↩✤✦✳↩✤✦✳↩✤✦✳↩✤✦✳↩✤✦✳↩✤✦✳↩✤✦✳↩✤✦✳↩✤✦✳↩✤✦✳

Introduction

✳

The trip which took all the courage and stamina of this brave English horsewoman in 1873 has now become a casual summer excursion for American families. What Isabella Bird called "no region for tourists and women" is today a popular resort, traversed by a highway carrying millions. The American motorist no longer seeks the kind of adventure she looked for. But the few thousand each year who leave their automobiles and walk back on the trails can still have a notion of what she found on her trip up Longs Peak only five years after it had been first climbed. This remarkable book can help us all recapture that peculiar mountain changelessness which has always fascinated men. Having covered our plains and valleys with highways, factories, and cities, having subdivided our hillsides into suburbs, having deepened and dammed up and rerouted our rivers to make seaways or sources of electric power, we have left only the ocean and the mountains to remind us of what we cannot do to the landscape.

Anyone who climbs Longs Peak this year or next will find the same Boulder Field, the same view of Chasm Lake, the same sheer East Face, the same slopes and cliffs on the north and the south, and, at the end, the same "grand well-defined mountain-top . . . a nearly level acre of boulders, with precipitous sides all round." All of us, even those who, like Isabella Bird, have been humiliated by being "dragged up, like a bale of goods" by our guide cannot forget the grand satisfaction of the view from the top. "From the summit were seen in unrivalled combination all the views which had rejoiced our eyes during the ascent. It was something at last to stand upon the storm-rent crown of this lonely sentinel of the Rocky Range, on one of the mightiest of the vertebrae of the backbone of the North American continent, and to see the waters start for both oceans. Uplifted above love and hate and storms of passion, calm amidst the eternal silences, fanned by zephyrs and bathed in living blue, peace rested for that one bright day on the Peak." All along the way on her rides from Longmont to Estes Park and back we recognize places today not noticeably different from when she rode there nearly a century ago. No one has better captured the iridescent changelessness of these mountains.

But this is more than a book of mountain travel. It is a record of speedily changing American life in the days when the West was most full of change. Isabella Bird's pen was doubly vivid because (as she casually notes) she often had to put her ink bottle on a corner of the cabin stove to thaw it for writing. This cultivated, cosmopolitan English lady writes with eloquent reticence of the passions of isolated settlers and miscellaneous refugees from civilization. "If one were compelled to live here in solitude," she wrote from "Nameless Region, Rocky Mountains, September," "one might truly say of the bears, deer, and elk which abound, 'Their tameness is shocking to me.' "

The tour of the Rockies which Isabella Bird describes in this volume was made during the autumn and early winter of 1873 on her way back to England from the Hawaiian Islands (then called the Sandwich Islands). Born at Boroughbridge Hall, Yorkshire, England in 1831, she inherited strong evangelical views from her father, an Anglican clergyman. She did her first traveling when, in her early twenties, she suffered from a spinal complaint, and a sea voyage was recommended for her health. She visited Prince Edward's Island, Canada, and the United States. At her father's suggestion she returned here a few years later, in 1857–58, to study the current religious revival. Upon her return to Great Britain she developed a charitable interest in the people of the West Highlands of Scotland. She went to live among them, helped organize their emigration to Canada (1862–66), and later visited Canada to see how they were getting on. Another journey to the Mediterranean and the eastern United States preceded the trip described in the present volume. When she set out for this trip, she was still suffering from ill health, which she hoped to improve by travel.

After returning to Great Britain from her Rocky Mountain tour of 1873, she studied the microscope and worked to found a college for medical missionaries. Her career as a world traveler had only begun. In 1878, she spent seven months in Japan traveling in the interior and five months in the Malay Peninsula. In 1889, she visited India and Tibet. About this time she conceived a plan (frustrated by the Turkish government) for a hospital at Nazareth. She had become a convert to missions, she explained, "not by missionary successes, but by seeing in four and a half years of Asiatic traveling the desperate needs of the un-Christianized world." She established the John Bishop Memorial Hospital in Kashmir and the Henrietta Bird Hospital for Women in the Punjab, and founded three more hospitals in China and Korea. Her travels continued, in Persia, Kurdistan, and elsewhere, into her late years. When in her middle sixties, she again toured Canada, Japan, Korea, and China, spending fifteen months and covering 8,000 miles in China alone. She died at Edinburgh in her seventy-third year.

It is hard to recall another woman in any age or country who traveled as widely, who saw so much, and who left so perceptive a record of what she saw. There was nothing faddish or snobbish, and very little that was romantic in her travel interests. She did not try to retrace the steps of famous adventurers before her. Unlike Richard Halliburton, she was not interested in following the track of Cortés, of Hannibal, or of Alexander the Great. Unlike John Lawson Stoddard or Burton Holmes, she did not go gathering raw material for entertaining lectures or travel books. Her writing was more often the by-product than the purpose of her trip. Strictly speaking, she was not an explorer or geographical discoverer. Yet the eminent British geographers of her day considered her one of themselves. In 1892, she became the first woman ever elected a Fellow of the Royal Geographical Society.

The contents of the present volume were first published serially as "Letters from the Rocky Mountains," in the genteel English weekly *Leisure Hour* in 1878—along with anecdotes on natural history, articles on "Taxation and the Working Classes," observations on fossil footprints, and remarks on "Female Education in China." They were first published in book form under the title, *A Lady's Life in the Rocky Mountains*, by John Murray of London in 1879. But G. P. Putnam's Sons, New York, had an edition out that same year, and by November 27, Isabella Bird was able to see a second edition,[1] and on January 16, 1880, still

[1] "These letters, as their style sufficiently indicates, were written without the remotest idea of publication. They appeared last year in the *Leisure Hour* at the request of its editor, and were so favor-

a third. Her slight notes of emendation for each of these editions appear in one copy I have seen. By 1882, the work was in its seventh edition; the last (eighth) edition, published by Putnam's, appeared in 1912. The book has been translated into French.

This was only one of many books by Isabella Bird. Each of her journeys produced at least one volume. All are still worth reading. She was an enthusiastic photographer, and carried the cumbersome apparatus of those days so that she could take her own pictures in remote places. Her books on China, Korea, and Japan show an extraordinary ability to wander off the beaten track of Western European thought. "We go forward with 'a light heart,' " she warned in *The Yangtze Valley and Beyond* (1900), "along with other European empires, not hesitating, for the sake of commercial advantages, to break up in the case of a fourth of the human race the most ancient of earth's existing civilizations, without giving any equivalent. . . . It is essential for us to see quite clearly that our Western ideas find themselves confronted, not with barbarism or with debased theories of morals, but with an elaborate and antique civilization which has many claims to our respect and even admiration."

In the Rockies, as in China and elsewhere, she never suffered from the tourist's nearsightedness. She avoided the romantic jargon of the professional world traveler. Nor was she confined by the specialized ways of observation that would later distinguish the professional anthropolo-

ably received that I venture to present them to the public in a separate form, as a record of very interesting traveling experiences, and of a phase of pioneer life which is rapidly passing away."— Publisher's prefatory note to the second edition.

gist. She had no list of items to check off when she arrived in a new country. She was not seeking curiosities to sate the provincial complacency of people back home. Her geographical knowledge, her feeling for shape and color, for flora and fauna, gave her writing an objective focus. Yet she always seemed most interested in discovering what it felt like to live in other places. She had an amazing capacity quickly to become a resident.

Isabella Bird's own cryptic explanation was that she traveled "for recreation and interest solely." Such an innocent, uncrusading traveler had a great deal to teach her countrymen in an age when they felt it "greatly to his credit" for anyone to be an Englishman. In the day of the "White Man's Burden," she had something to say that could not be found in Kipling or Disraeli or Gladstone. For she could live among the oddest people—pagan Chinese and uncouth Americans—without being either shocked or "charmed" by their un-English ways.

Almost always Isabella Bird traveled alone. Yet she seldom complained of loneliness nor did she tell us much of her personal feelings. She remained extremely close to her only sister, Henrietta, with whom she lived in the intervals between travels. Several of her books, including the present one, were written as letters to her sister. In 1881, the year after Henrietta's death, when Isabella was herself fifty, she married Dr. John Bishop (ten years her junior), who had been Henrietta's physician. He died only five years later. The most tantalizing part of the present volume is the half-told story of her affection for Mountain Jim.

During the years of Isabella Bird's travels, the United States was a common destination for well-to-do Europeans, and especially for Englishmen seeking adventure without undue risk. Many came here and many wrote books—famous authors like Charles Dickens and Anthony Trollope as well as unknown businessmen and house-wives, long-term residents like Fanny Kemble, and people passing through like Isabella Bird. In the mid-nineteenth century, literate English men and women were no more reticent to publish generalizations about "America" or "Americans" after a few weeks in New York or New Orleans, than are Americans nowadays to describe "Russia" after a few days in Moscow. It was an age of uncritical generalizations, especially by Englishmen and about Americans.

Isabella Bird was well aware of these irritating generalizing ways of her countrymen and was determined not to share them. "A celebrated hunter, Bob Craik," she wrote from Hall's Gulch, Colorado, "came in to supper with a young man in tow, whom, in spite of his rough hunter's or miner's dress, I at once recognized as an English gentleman. . . . This gentleman was lording it in true caricature fashion, with a Lord Dundreary drawl and a general execration of everything; while I sat in the chimney corner, speculating on the reason why many of the upper class of my countrymen—'High Toners,' as they are called out here—make themselves so ludicrously absurd. They neither know how to hold their tongues or to carry their personal pretensions. An American is nationally assumptive, an Englishman personally so. He took no notice of me till something passed which showed him I was English, when his manner at once changed into courtesy, and his drawl was shortened by a half. He took pains to let me know that he was an officer in the Guards, of good family, on four months' leave, which he was spending in slaying buffalo and elk, and also that he had a profound contempt for everything American."

The scarcity of inns and the common practice of taking in transients for the night gave her an intimate view of the "Wild West" (as she called it). Nothing is more impressive than her feeling for the nuance and variety of that life. She saw and noted the opposites of which life everywhere is made. She saw some cabins thick with filth, where food flecked with flies was served from a common greasy pan, and she saw others neat as a London parlor. She saw a society where, in a sense, everyone was young, yet where the most painful sight was "the extinction of childhood. I have never seen any children, only debased imitations of men and women." She saw a world of vigilance committees, lynchings, and desperados quick on the trigger, who would shoot a friend for an "impertinent remark." Yet she carefully noted that there were "few flagrant breaches of morality." Bricks of silver could be safely left unattended in a wagon on the street of a mining town; life and property, she said, were generally safer in Colorado than in England. She found a brutish sullenness in public places and a shocking crudity of table manners; yet nowhere did she fail to find gentleness or chivalry. She reported that her desperado-companion, Mountain Jim, had ridden sixty miles to find a doctor for a sick child. She found an oppressive lack of privacy amid the exhilarating solitudes of the wild mountains. She found people pinchpenny, parsimonious, greedy, yet willing to share their short rations or escort her on horseback hundreds of miles through a snowstorm.

Again and again in mountain villages she felt the overwhelming monotony of "a life in which nothing ever happens," yet in these same places—whenever she could see the mountain ranges and breathe the thin air—she found exuberant novelty in every moment. She noticed an incorrigible indolence among the very people who lived by "work, work, work . . . hard, loveless, moral." She found relentless temperance colonies alongside towns where the saloon was the community center. She saw a landscape where everyone talked of "progress," yet all was dominated by changeless mountains.

Isabella Bird luxuriated in the paradoxes of this world: an English lady wearing Hawaiian riding dress, mounted on Birdie, her borrowed pony, guided by the one-eyed desperado Mountain Jim, entertaining her with his recitations of poetry and cultivated conversation. Her Rocky Mountain adventure symbolized that improbable combination of opposites which was the American West, and which was perhaps the most American aspect of that West.

DANIEL J. BOORSTIN

A Lady's Life
in the Rocky Mountains

Letter I

✳

✦❀✦❀✦❀✦❀✦❀✦❀✦❀✦❀✦❀✦❀✦❀✦❀✦❀

✦❀✦❀✦❀✦❀✦❀✦❀✦❀✦❀✦❀✦❀✦❀✦❀✦❀

Lake Tahoe, *September 2.*

I have found a dream of beauty at which one might look
all one's life and sigh. Not lovable, like the Sandwich
Islands, but beautiful in its own way! A strictly North
American beauty—snow-splotched mountains, huge pines,
red-woods, sugar pines, silver spruce; a crystalline atmosphere, waves of the richest color; and a pine-hung lake
which mirrors all beauty on its surface. Lake Tahoe is before me, a sheet of water twenty-two miles long by ten
broad, and in some places 1,700 feet deep. It lies at a height
of 6,000 feet, and the snow-crowned summits which wall
it in are from 8,000 to 11,000 feet in altitude. The air is
keen and elastic. There is no sound but the distant and
slightly musical ring of the lumberer's axe.

It is a weariness to go back, even in thought, to the clang
of San Francisco, which I left in its cold morning fog early
yesterday, driving to the Oakland ferry through streets
with side-walks heaped with thousands of cantaloupe
and water-melons, tomatoes, cucumbers, squashes, pears,
grapes, peaches, apricots—all of startling size as compared

3

with any I ever saw before. Other streets were piled with
sacks of flour, left out all night, owing to the security
from rain at this season. I pass hastily over the early part
of the journey, the crossing the bay in a fog as chill as
November, the number of "lunch baskets," which gave
the car the look of conveying a great picnic party, the
last view of the Pacific, on which I had looked for nearly
a year, the fierce sunshine and brilliant sky inland, the look
of long *rainlessness*, which one may not call drought, the
valleys with sides crimson with the poison oak, the dusty
vineyards, with great purple clusters thick among the
leaves, and between the vines great dusty melons lying on
the dusty earth. From off the boundless harvest fields the
grain was carried in June, and it is now stacked in sacks
along the track, awaiting freightage. California is a "land
flowing with milk and honey." The barns are bursting
with fullness. In the dusty orchards the apple and pear
branches are supported, that they may not break down
under the weight of fruit; melons, tomatoes, and squashes
of gigantic size lie almost unheeded on the ground; fat
cattle, gorged almost to repletion, shade themselves under
the oaks; superb "red" horses shine, not with grooming,
but with condition; and thriving farms everywhere show
on what a solid basis the prosperity of the "Golden State"
is founded. Very uninviting, however rich, was the blazing Sacramento Valley, and very repulsive the city of
Sacramento, which, at a distance of 125 miles from the
Pacific, has an elevation of only thirty feet. The mercury
stood at 103° in the shade, and the fine white dust was
stifling.

In the late afternoon we began the ascent of the Sierras,
whose sawlike points had been in sight for many miles.

The dusty fertility was all left behind, the country became rocky and gravelly, and deeply scored by streams bearing the muddy wash of the mountain gold mines down to the muddier Sacramento. There were long broken ridges and deep ravines, the ridges becoming longer, the ravines deeper, the pines thicker and larger, as we ascended into a cool atmosphere of exquisite purity, and before six P.M. the last traces of cultivation and the last hardwood trees were left behind.[1]

At Colfax, a station at a height of 2,400 feet, I got out and walked the length of the train. First came two great gaudy engines, the Grizzly Bear and the White Fox, with their respective tenders loaded with logs of wood, the engines with great, solitary, reflecting lamps in front above the cow guards, a quantity of polished brass-work, comfortable glass houses, and well-stuffed seats for the engine-drivers. The engines and tenders were succeeded by a baggage car, the latter loaded with bullion and valuable parcels, and in charge of two "express agents." Each of these cars is forty-five feet long. Then came two cars loaded with peaches and grapes; then two "silver palace" cars, each sixty feet long; then a smoking car, at that time occupied mainly by Chinamen; and then five ordinary

[1] In consequence of the unobserved omission of a date to my letters having been pointed out to me, I take this opportunity of stating that I traveled in Colorado in the autumn and early winter of 1873, on my way to England from the Sandwich Islands. The letters are a faithful picture of the country and state of society as it then was; but friends who have returned from the West within the last six months tell me that things are rapidly changing, that the frame house is replacing the log cabin, and that the footprints of elk and bighorn may be sought for in vain on the dewy slopes of Estes Park. I. L. B. (Author's note to the third edition, January 16, 1880.)

passenger cars, with platforms like all the others, making altogether a train about 700 feet in length.

The platforms of the four front cars were clustered over with Digger Indians, with their squaws, children, and gear. They are perfect savages, without any aptitude for even aboriginal civilization, and are altogether the most degraded of the ill-fated tribes which are dying out before the white races. They were all very diminutive, five feet one inch being, I should think, about the average height, with flat noses, wide mouths, and black hair, cut straight above the eyes and hanging lank and long at the back and sides. The squaws wore their hair thickly plastered with pitch, and a broad band of the same across their noses and cheeks. They carried their infants on their backs, strapped to boards. The clothing of both sexes was a ragged, dirty combination of coarse woolen cloth and hide, the moccasins being unornamented. They were all hideous and filthy, and swarming with vermin. The men carried short bows and arrows, one of them, who appeared to be the chief, having a lynx's skin for a quiver. A few had fishing tackle, but the bystanders said that they lived almost entirely upon grasshoppers. They were a most impressive incongruity in the midst of the tokens of an omnipotent civilization.

The light of the sinking sun from that time glorified the Sierras, and as the dew fell, aromatic odors made the still air sweet. On a single track, sometimes carried on a narrow ledge excavated from the mountain side by men lowered from the top in baskets, overhanging ravines from 2,000 to 3,000 feet deep, the monster train *snaked* its way upwards, stopping sometimes in front of a few frame houses, at others where nothing was to be seen but a log cabin with a few Chinamen hanging about it, but where trails on the sides of the ravines pointed to a gold country above and below. So sharp and frequent are the curves on some parts of the ascent, that on looking out of the window one could seldom see more than a part of the train at once. At Cape Horn, where the track curves round the ledge of a precipice 2,500 feet in depth, it is correct to be frightened, and a fashion of holding the breath and shutting the eyes prevails, but my fears were reserved for the crossing of a trestle bridge over a very deep chasm, which is itself approached by a sharp curve. This bridge appeared to be overlapped by the cars so as to produce the effect of looking down directly into a wild gulch, with a torrent raging along it at an immense depth below.

Shivering in the keen, frosty air near the summit pass of the Sierras, we entered the "snow-sheds," wooden galleries, which for about fifty miles shut out all the splendid views of the region, as given in dioramas, not even allowing a glimpse of "the Gem of the Sierras," the lovely Donner Lake. One of these sheds is twenty-seven miles long. In a few hours the mercury had fallen from 103° to 29°, and we had ascended 6,987 feet in 105 miles! After passing through the sheds, we had several grand views of a pine forest on fire before reaching Truckee at 11 P.M., having traveled 258 miles. Truckee, the center of the "lumbering region" of the Sierras, is usually spoken of as "a rough mountain town," and Mr. W. had told me that all the roughs of the district congregated there, that there were nightly pistol affrays in bar-rooms, etc., but as he admitted that a lady was sure of respect, and Mr. G. strongly advised me to stay and see the lakes, I got out, much dazed, and very stupid with sleep, envying the people in the sleeping car, who were already unconscious on their luxurious couches. The cars drew up in a street—if street that could be called which was only a wide, cleared space, intersected by rails, with here and there a stump, and great piles of sawn logs bulking big in the moonlight, and a number of irregular clap-board, steep-roofed houses, many of them with open fronts, glaring with light and crowded with men. We had pulled up at the door of a rough Western hotel, with a partially open front, being a bar-room crowded with men drinking and smoking, and the space between it and the cars was a moving mass of loafers and passengers. On the tracks, engines, tolling heavy bells, were mightily moving, the glare from their cyclopean eyes dulling the light of a forest which was burning fitfully on a mountain side; and on open spaces great fires of pine logs were burning cheerily, with groups of men round them. A band was playing noisily, and the unholy sound of tom-toms was not far off. Mountains— the Sierras of many a fireside dream—seemed to wall in the town, and great pines stood out, sharp and clear cut, against a sky in which a moon and stars were shining frostily.

It was a sharp frost at that great height, and when an "irrepressible nigger," who seemed to represent the hotel establishment, deposited me and my carpetbag in a room which answered for "the parlor," I was glad to find some remains of pine knots still alight in the stove. A man came in and said that when the cars were gone he would try to get me a room, but they were so full that it would be a very poor one. The crowd was solely masculine. It was then 11:30 P.M., and I had not had a meal since 6 A.M.; but when I asked hopefully for a hot supper, with tea, I was told that no supper could be got at that hour; but in half

8

an hour the same man returned with a small cup of cold, weak tea, and a small slice of bread, which looked as if it had been much handled.

I asked the Negro factotum about the hire of horses, and presently a man came in from the bar who, he said, could supply my needs. This man, the very type of a Western pioneer, bowed, threw himself into a rocking-chair, drew a spittoon beside him, cut a fresh quid of tobacco, began to chew energetically, and put his feet, cased in miry high boots, into which his trousers were tucked, on the top of the stove. He said he had horses which would both "lope" and trot, that some ladies preferred the Mexican saddle, that I could ride alone in perfect safety; and after a route had been devised, I hired a horse for two days. This man wore a pioneer's badge as one of the earliest settlers of California, but he had moved on as one place after another had become too civilized for him, "but nothing," he added, "was likely to change much in Truckee." I was afterwards told that the usual regular hours of sleep are not observed there. The accommodation is too limited for the population of 2,000,[2] which is masculine mainly, and is liable to frequent temporary additions, and beds are occupied continuously, though by different occupants, throughout the greater part of the twenty-four hours. Consequently I found the bed and room allotted to me quite tumbled looking. Men's coats and sticks were hanging up, miry boots were littered about, and a rifle was in one corner. There was no window to the outer air, but I slept soundly, being only once awoke by an increase of the same din in which I had fallen asleep, varied by three pistol shots fired in rapid succession.

[2] *Nelson's Guide to the Central Pacific Railroad.*

This morning Truckee wore a totally different aspect. The crowds of the night before had disappeared. There were heaps of ashes where the fires had been. A sleepy German waiter seemed the only person about the premises, the open drinking saloons were nearly empty, and only a few sleepy-looking loafers hung about in what is called the street. It might have been Sunday; but they say that it brings a great accession of throng and jollity. Public worship has died out at present; work is discontinued on Sunday, but the day is given up to pleasure. Putting a minimum of indispensables into a bag, and slipping on my Hawaiian riding dress[3] over a silk skirt, and a dust cloak over all, I stealthily crossed the plaza to the livery stable, the largest building in Truckee, where twelve fine horses were stabled in stalls on each side of a broad drive. My friend of the evening before showed me his "rig," three velvet-covered side-saddles almost without horns. Some ladies, he said, used the horn of the Mexican saddle, but none "in the part" rode cavalier fashion. I felt abashed. I could not ride any distance in the conventional mode, and was just going to give up this splendid "ravage," when the man said, "Ride your own fashion; here, at Truckee, if anywhere in the world, people can do as they like." Blissful Truckee! In no time a large grey horse was "rigged out" in a handsome silver-bossed Mexican saddle, with ornamental leather tassels hanging from the stirrup guards,

[3] For the benefit of other lady travelers, I wish to explain that my "Hawaiian riding dress" is the "American Lady's Mountain Dress," a half-fitting jacket, a skirt reaching to the ankles, and full Turkish trousers gathered into frills falling over the boots,—a thoroughly serviceable and feminine costume for mountaineering and other rough traveling, as in the Alps or any other part of the world. I. L. B. (Author's note to the second edition, November 27, 1879.)

and a housing of black bear's-skin. I strapped my silk skirt on the saddle, deposited my cloak in the corn-bin, and was safely on the horse's back before his owner had time to devise any way of mounting me. Neither he nor any of the loafers who had assembled showed the slightest sign of astonishment, but all were as respectful as possible.

Once on horseback my embarrassment disappeared, and I rode through Truckee, whose irregular, steep-roofed houses and shanties, set down in a clearing and surrounded closely by mountain and forest, looked like a temporary encampment; passed under the Pacific Railroad; and then for twelve miles followed the windings of the Truckee River, a clear, rushing, mountain stream, in which immense pine logs had gone aground not to be floated off till the next freshet, a loud-tongued, rollicking stream of ice-cold water, on whose banks no ferns or trailers hang, and which leaves no greenness along its turbulent progress. All was bright with that brilliancy of sky and atmosphere, that blaze of sunshine and universal glitter, which I never saw till I came to California, combined with an elasticity in the air which removed all lassitude, and gives one spirit enough for anything. On either side of the Truckee great sierras rose like walls, castellated, embattled, rifted, skirted and crowned with pines of enormous size, the walls now and then breaking apart to show some snow-slashed peak rising into a heaven of intense, unclouded, sunny blue. At this altitude of 6,000 feet one must learn to be content with varieties of Coniferae, for, except for aspens, which spring up in some places where the pines have been cleared away, and for cotton-woods, which at a lower level fringe the streams, there is nothing but the bear cherry, the raspberry, the gooseberry, the wild grape, and the wild currant. None of these grew near the Truckee, but I feasted my eyes on pines[4] which, though not so large as the Wellingtonia of the Yosemite, are really gigantic, attaining a height of 250 feet, their huge stems, the warm red of cedar wood, rising straight and branchless for a third of their height, their diameter from seven to fifteen feet, their shape that of a larch, but with the needles long and dark, and cones a foot long. Pines cleft the sky; they were massed wherever level ground occurred; they stood over the Truckee at right angles, or lay across it in prostrate grandeur. Their stumps and carcasses were everywhere; and smooth "shoots" on the sierras marked where they were shot down as "felled timber," to be floated off by the river. To them this wild region owes its scattered population, and the sharp ring of the lumberer's axe mingles with the cries of wild beasts and the roar of mountain torrents.

The track is a soft, natural, wagon road, very pleasant to ride on. The horse was much too big for me, and had plans of his own; but now and then, where the ground admitted to it, I tried his heavy "lope" with much amusement. I met nobody, and passed nothing on the road but a freight wagon, drawn by twenty-two oxen, guided by three fine-looking men, who had some difficulty in making room for me to pass their awkward convoy. After I had ridden about ten miles the road went up a steep hill in the forest, turned abruptly, and through the blue gloom of the great pines which rose from the ravine in which the river was then hid, came glimpses of two mountains, about 11,000 feet in height, whose bald grey summits were crowned with pure snow. It was one of those glorious sur-

[4] *Pinus Lambertina.*

prises in scenery which make one feel as if one must bow down and worship. The forest was thick, and had an undergrowth of dwarf spruce and brambles, but as the horse had become fidgety and "scary" on the track, I turned off in the idea of taking a short cut, and was sitting carelessly, shortening my stirrup, when a great, dark, hairy beast rose, crashing and snorting, out of the tangle just in front of me. I had only a glimpse of him, and thought that my imagination had magnified a wild boar, but it was a bear. The horse snorted and plunged violently, as if he would go down to the river, and then turned, still plunging, up a steep bank, when, finding that I must come off, I threw myself off on the right side, where the ground rose considerably, so that I had not far to fall. I got up covered with dust, but neither shaken nor bruised. It was truly grotesque and humiliating. The bear ran in one direction, and the horse in another. I hurried after the latter, and twice he stopped till I was close to him, then turned round and cantered away. After walking about a mile in deep dust, I picked up first the saddle-blanket and next my bag, and soon came upon the horse, standing facing me, and shaking all over. I thought I should catch him then, but when I went up to him he turned round, threw up his heels several times, rushed off the track, galloped in circles, bucking, kicking, and plunging for some time, and then throwing up his heels as an act of final defiance, went off at full speed in the direction of Truckee, with the saddle over his shoulders and the great wooden stirrups thumping his sides, while I trudged ignominiously along in the dust, laboriously carrying the bag and saddle-blanket.

I walked for nearly an hour, heated and hungry, when

to my joy I saw the ox-team halted across the top of a gorge, and one of the teamsters leading the horse towards me. The young man said that, seeing the horse coming, they had drawn the team across the road to stop him, and remembering that he had passed them with a lady on him, they feared that there had been an accident, and had just saddled one of their own horses to go in search of me. He brought me some water to wash the dust from my face, and re-saddled the horse, but the animal snorted and plunged for some time before he would let me mount, and then sidled along in such a nervous and scared way, that the teamster walked for some distance by me to see that I was "all right." He said that the woods in the neighborhood of Tahoe had been full of brown and grizzly bears for some days, but that no one was in any danger from them. I took a long gallop beyond the scene of my tumble to quiet the horse, who was most restless and troublesome.

Then the scenery became truly magnificent and bright with life. Crested blue-jays darted through the dark pines, squirrels in hundreds scampered through the forest, red dragon-flies flashed like "living light," exquisite chipmonks ran across the track, but only a dusty blue lupin here and there reminded me of earth's fairer children. Then the river became broad and still, and mirrored in its transparent depths regal pines, straight as an arrow, with rich yellow and green lichen clinging to their stems, and firs and balsam pines filling up the spaces between them, the gorge opened, and this mountain-girdled lake lay before me, with its margin broken up into bays and promontories, most picturesquely clothed by huge sugar pines. It lay dimpling and scintillating beneath the noonday sun, as entirely unspoilt as fifteen years ago, when its pure loveliness was known only to trappers and Indians. One man lives on it the whole year round; otherwise early October strips its shores of their few inhabitants, and thereafter, for seven months, it is rarely accessible except on snow-shoes. It never freezes. In the dense forests which bound it, and drape two-thirds of its gaunt sierras, are hordes of grizzlies, brown bears, wolves, elk, deer, chipmonks, mar-tens, minks, skunks, foxes, squirrels, and snakes. On its margin I found an irregular wooden inn, with a lumber-wagon at the door, on which was the carcass of a large grizzly bear, shot behind the house this morning. I had intended to ride ten miles farther, but, finding that the trail in some places was a "blind" one, and being bewitched by the beauty and serenity of Tahoe, I have remained here sketching, reveling in the view from the veranda, and strolling in the forest. At this height there is frost every night of the year, and my fingers are benumbed.

The beauty is entrancing. The sinking sun is out of sight behind the western Sierras, and all the pine-hung promontories on this side of the water are rich indigo, just reddened with lake, deepening here and there into Tyrian purple. The peaks above, which still catch the sun, are bright rose-red, and all the mountains on the other side are pink; and pink, too, are the far-off summits on which the snow-drifts rest. Indigo, red, and orange tints stain the still water, which lies solemn and dark against the shore, under the shadow of stately pines. An hour later, and a moon nearly full—not a pale, flat disc, but a radiant sphere —has wheeled up into the flushed sky. The sunset has passed through every stage of beauty, through every glory of color, through riot and triumph, through pathos and tenderness, into a long, dreamy, painless rest, succeeded by the profound solemnity of the moonlight, and a stillness broken only by the night cries of beasts in the aromatic forests.

I. L. B.

Letter II

✳

✤✦✱✦✤✦✱✦✤✦✱✦✤✦✱✦✤✦✱✦✤✦✱✦✤✦✱✦✤✦✱✦✤✦

A LADY'S "GET-UP"—GRIZZLY BEARS—THE "GEM OF
THE SIERRAS"—A TRAGIC TALE—A CARNIVAL OF COLOR.

✤✦✱✦✤✦✱✦✤✦✱✦✤✦✱✦✤✦✱✦✤✦✱✦✤✦✱✦✤✦✱✦✤✦

CHEYENNE, WYOMING, *September* 7.

As night came on the cold intensified, and the stove in the
parlor attracted every one. A San Francisco lady, much
"got up" in paint, emerald green velvet, Brussels lace, and
diamonds, rattled continuously for the amusement of the
company, giving descriptions of persons and scenes in a
racy Western twang, without the slightest scruple as to
what she said. In a few years Tahoe will be inundated in
summer with similar vulgarity, owing to its easiness of
access. I sustained the reputation which our country-
women bear in America by looking a "perfect guy"; and
feeling that I was a salient point for the speaker's next
sally, I was relieved when the landlady, a ladylike Englishwoman, asked me to join herself and her family in the
bar-room, where we had much talk about the neighborhood and its wild beasts, especially bears. The forest is full
of them, but they seem never to attack people unless when
wounded, or much aggravated by dogs, or a shebear thinks
you are going to molest her young.

I dreamt of bears so vividly that I woke with a furry
death hug at my throat, but feeling quite refreshed. When
I mounted my horse after breakfast the sun was high and
the air so keen and intoxicating that, giving the animal his

head, I galloped up and down hill, feeling completely tire-less. Truly, that air is the elixir of life. I had a glorious ride back to Truckee. The road was not as solitary as the day before. In a deep part of the forest the horse snorted and reared, and I saw a cinnamon-colored bear with two cubs cross the track ahead of me. I tried to keep the horse quiet that the mother might acquit me of any designs upon her lolloping children, but I was glad when the ungainly, long-haired party crossed the river. Then I met a team, the driver of which stopped and said he was glad that I had not gone to Cornelian Bay, it was such a bad trail, and hoped I had enjoyed Tahoe. The driver of another team stopped and asked if I had seen any bears. Then a man heavily armed, a hunter probably, asked me if I were the English tourist who had "happened on" a "Grizzly" yesterday. Then I saw a lumberer taking his dinner on a rock in the river, who "touched his hat" and brought me a draught of ice-cold water, which I could hardly drink owing to the fractiousness of the horse, and gathered me some mountain pinks, which I admired. I mention these little incidents to indicate the habit of respectful courtesy to women which prevails in that region. These men might have been excused for speaking in a somewhat free-and-easy tone to a lady riding alone, and in an unwonted fashion. Womanly dignity and manly respect for women are the salt of society in this wild West.

My horse was so excitable that I avoided the center of Truckee, and skulked through a collection of Chinamen's shanties to the stable, where a prodigious roan horse, standing seventeen hands high, was produced for my ride to the Donner Lake. I asked the owner, who was as interested in my enjoying myself as a West Highlander might have been, if there were not ruffians about who might make an evening ride dangerous. A story was current of a man having ridden through Truckee two evenings before with a chopped-up human body in a sack behind the saddle, and hosts of stories of ruffianism are located there, rightly or wrongly. This man said, "There's a bad breed of ruffians, but the ugliest among them all won't touch you. There's nothing Western folk admire so much as pluck in a woman." I had to get on a barrel before I could reach the stirrup, and when I was mounted my feet only came half-way down the horse's sides. I felt like a fly on him. The road at first lay through a valley without a river, but some swampishness nourished some rank swamp grass, the first *green* grass I have seen in America; and the pines, with their red stems, looked beautiful rising out of it. I hurried along, and came upon the Donner Lake quite suddenly, to be completely smitten by its beauty. It is only about three miles long by one and a half broad, and lies hidden away among mountains, with no dwellings on its shores but some deserted lumberers' cabins.[1] Its loneliness pleased me well. I did not see man, beast, or bird from the time I left Truckee till I returned. The mountains, which rise abruptly from the margin, are covered with dense pine forests, through which, here and there, strange forms of bare grey rock, castellated, or needle-like, protrude themselves. On the opposite side, at a height of about 6,000 feet, a grey, ascending line, from which rumbling, incoherent sounds occasionally proceeded, is seen through the pines. This is one of the snow-sheds of the Pacific Railroad, which shuts out from travelers all that I was seeing.

[1] Visitors can now be accommodated at a tolerable mountain hotel.

The lake is called after Mr. Donner, who, with his family, arrived at the Truckee River in the fall of the year, in company with a party of emigrants bound for California. Being encumbered with many cattle, he let the company pass on, and, with his own party of sixteen souls, which included his wife and four children, encamped by the lake. In the morning they found themselves surrounded by an expanse of snow, and after some consultation it was agreed that the whole party except Mr. Donner who was unwell, his wife, and a German friend, should take the horses and attempt to cross the mountain, which, after much peril, they succeeded in doing; but, as the storm continued for several weeks, it was impossible for any rescue party to succor the three who had been left behind. In the early spring, when the snow was hard enough for traveling, a party started in quest, expecting to find the snow-bound alive and well, as they had cattle enough for their support, and, after weeks of toil and exposure, they scaled the Sierras and reached the Donner Lake. On arriving at the camp they opened the rude door, and there, sitting before the fire, they found the German, holding a roasted human arm and hand, which he was greedily eating. The rescue party overpowered him, and with difficulty tore the arm from him. A short search discovered the body of the lady, minus the arm, frozen in the snow, round, plump, and fair, showing that she was in perfect health when she met her fate. The rescuers returned to California, taking the German with them, whose story was that Mr. Donner died in the fall, and that the cattle escaped, leaving them but little food, and that when this was exhausted Mrs. Donner died. The story never gained any credence, and the truth oozed out that the German had murdered the husband, then brutally murdered the wife, and had seized upon Donner's money. There were, however, no witnesses, and the murderer escaped with the enforced surrender of the money to the Donner orphans.

This tragic story filled my mind as I rode towards the head of the lake, which became every moment grander and more unutterably lovely. The sun was setting fast, and against his golden light green promontories, wooded with stately pines, stood out one beyond another in a medium of dark rich blue, while grey bleached summits, peaked, turreted, and snow slashed, were piled above them, gleaming with amber light. Darker grew the blue gloom, the dew fell heavily, aromatic odors floated on the air, and still the lofty peaks glowed with living light, till in one second it died off from them, leaving them with the ashy paleness of a dead face. It was dark and cold under the mountain shadows, the frosty chill of the high altitude wrapped me round, the solitude was overwhelming, and I reluctantly turned my horse's head towards Truckee, often looking back to the ashy summits in their unearthly fascination. Eastwards the look of the scenery was changing every moment, while the lake for long remained "one burnished sheet of living gold," and Truckee lay utterly out of sight in a hollow filled with lake and cobalt. Before long a carnival of color began which I can only describe as delirious, intoxicating, a hardly bearable joy, a tender anguish, an indescribable yearning, an unearthly music, rich in love and worship. It lasted considerably more than an hour, and though the road was growing very dark, and the train which was to take me thence was fast climbing the Sierras, I could not ride faster than a walk.

The eastward mountains, which had been grey, blushed

pale pink, the pink deepened into rose, and the rose into crimson, and then all solidity etherealized away and became clear and pure as an amethyst, while all the waving ranges and the broken pine-clothed ridges below etherealized too, but into a dark rich blue, and a strange effect of atmosphere blended the whole into one perfect picture. It changed, deepened, reddened, melted, growing more and more wonderful, while under the pines it was night, till, having displayed itself for an hour, the jewelled peaks suddenly became like those of the Sierras, wan as the face of death. Far later the cold golden light lingered in the west, with pines in relief against its purity, and where the rose light had glowed in the east, a huge moon unheaved itself, and the red flicker of forest fires luridly streaked the mountain sides near and far off. I realized that night had come with its *eeriness*, and putting my great horse into a gallop I clung on to him till I pulled him up in Truckee, which was at the height of its evening revelries—fires blazing out of doors, bar-rooms and saloons crammed, lights glaring, gaming tables thronged, fiddle and banjo in frightful discord, and the air ringing with ribaldry and profanity.

I. L. B.

Letter III

✳

❧✿✦❧✿✦❧✿✦❧✿✦❧✿✦❧✿✦❧✿✦❧✿✦❧✿✦❧✿✦❧✿✦❧✿✦❧✿✦❧✿✦❧✿✦

A Temple of Morpheus—Utah—A "God-forgotten" town—A distressed couple—Dog villages—A
temperance colony—A Colorado inn—The bug
pest—Fort Collins.

❧✿✦❧✿✦❧✿✦❧✿✦❧✿✦❧✿✦❧✿✦❧✿✦❧✿✦❧✿✦❧✿✦❧✿✦❧✿✦❧✿✦❧✿✦

Cheyenne, Wyoming, *September 8.*

Precisely at 11 p.m. the huge Pacific train, with its heavy
bell tolling, thundered up to the door of the Truckee
House, and on presenting my ticket at the double door of
a "Silver Palace" car, the slippered steward, whispering
low, conducted me to my berth—a luxurious bed three and
a half feet wide, with a hair mattress on springs, fine linen
sheets, and costly California blankets. The twenty-four
inmates of the car were all invisible, asleep behind rich
curtains. It was a true Temple of Morpheus. Profound
sleep was the object to which everything was dedicated.
Four silver lamps hanging from the roof, and burning low,
gave a dreamy light. On each side of the center passage,
rich rep curtains, green and crimson, striped with gold,
hung from silver bars running near the roof, and trailed
on the soft Axminster carpet. The temperature was carefully kept at 70°. It was 29° outside. Silence and freedom
from jolting were secured by double doors and windows,
costly and ingenious arrangements of springs and cush-
ions, and a speed limited to eighteen miles an hour.

As I lay down, the gallop under the dark pines, the

23

frosty moon, the forest fires, the flaring lights and roaring din of Truckee faded as dreams fade, and eight hours later a pure, pink dawn divulged a level blasted region, with grey sage brush growing out of a soil encrusted with alkali, and bounded on either side by low glaring ridges. All through that day we traveled under a cloudless sky over solitary glaring plains, and stopped twice at solitary, glaring frame houses, where coarse, greasy meals, infested by lazy flies, were provided at a dollar per head. By evening we were running across the continent on a bee line, and I sat for an hour on the rear platform of the rear car to enjoy the wonderful beauty of the sunset and the atmosphere. Far as one could see in the crystalline air there was nothing but desert. The jagged Humboldt ranges flaming in the sunset, with snow in their clefts, though forty-five miles off, looked within an easy canter. The bright metal track, purpling like all else in the cool distance, was all that linked one with Eastern or Western civilization.

The next morning, when the steward unceremoniously turned us out of our berths soon after sunrise, we were running down upon the Great Salt Lake, bounded by the white Wahsatch ranges. Along its shores, by means of irrigation, Mormon industry has compelled the ground to yield fine crops of hay and barley; and we passed several cabins, from which, even at that early hour, Mormons, each with two or three wives, were going forth to their day's work. The women were ugly, and their shapeless blue dresses hideous. At the Mormon town of Ogden we changed cars, and again traversed dusty plains, white and glaring, varied by muddy streams and rough, arid valleys, now and then narrowing into canyons. By common consent the windows were kept closed to exclude the fine white alkaline dust, which is very irritating to the nostrils. The journey became more and more wearisome as we ascended rapidly over immense plains and wastes of gravel destitute of mountain boundaries, and with only here and there a "knob" or "butte"[1] to break the monotony. The wheel-marks of the trail to Utah often ran parallel with the track, and bones of oxen were bleaching in the sun, the remains of those "whose carcasses fell in the wilderness" on the long and drouthy journey. The daybreak of to-day (Sunday) found us shivering at Fort Laramie, a frontier post dismally situated at a height of 7,000 feet. Another 1,000 feet over gravelly levels brought us to Sherman, the highest level reached by this railroad. From this point eastward the streams fall into the Atlantic. The ascent of these apparently level plateaus is called "crossing the Rocky Mountains," but I have seen nothing of the range, except two peaks like teeth lying low on the distant horizon. It became mercilessly cold; some people thought it snowed, but I only saw rolling billows of fog. Lads passed through the cars the whole morning, selling newspapers, novels, cacti, lollypops, pop corn, pea nuts, and ivory ornaments, so that, having lost all reckoning of the days, I never knew that it was Sunday till the cars pulled up at the door of the hotel in this detestable place.

The surrounding plains were endless and verdureless. The scanty grasses were long ago turned into sun-cured hay by the fierce summer heats. There is neither tree nor bush, the sky is grey, the earth buff, the air *blae* and windy, and clouds of coarse granitic dust sweep across the prairie

[1] The mountains which bound the "valley of the Babbling Waters," Utah, afford striking examples of these "knobs" or "buttes."

and smother the settlement. Cheyenne is described as "a God-forsaken, God-forgotten place." That it forgets God is written on its face. It owes its existence to the railroad, and has diminished in population, but is a depôt for a large amount of the necessaries of life which are distributed through the scantily settled districts within distances of 300 miles by "freight wagons," each drawn by four or six horses or mules, or double that number of oxen. At times over 100 wagons, with double that number of teamsters, are in Cheyenne at once. A short time ago it was a perfect pandemonium, mainly inhabited by rowdies and desperadoes, the scum of advancing civilization; and murders, stabbings, shootings, and pistol affrays were at times events of almost hourly occurrence in its drinking dens. But in the West, when things reach their worst, a sharp and sure remedy is provided. Those settlers who find the state of matters intolerable, organize themselves into a Vigilance Committee. "Judge Lynch," with a few feet of rope, appears on the scene, the majority crystallizes round the supporters of order, warnings are issued to obnoxious people, simply bearing a scrawl of a tree with a man dangling from it, with such words as "Clear out of this by 6 A.M., or ———." A number of the worst desperadoes are tried by a yet more summary process than a drumhead court-martial, "strung up," and buried ignominiously. I have been told that 120 ruffians were disposed of in this way here in a single fortnight. Cheyenne is now as safe as Hilo, and the interval between the most desperate lawlessness and the time when United States law, with its corruption and feebleness, comes upon the scene is one of comparative security and good order. Piety is not the *forte* of

Cheyenne. The roads resound with atrocious profanity, and the rowdyism of the saloons and bar-rooms is repressed, not extirpated.

The population, once 6,000, is now about 4,000. It is an ill-arranged set of frame houses and shanties;[2] and rubbish heaps, and offal of deer and antelope, produce the foulest smells I have smelt for a long time. Some of the houses are painted a blinding white; others are unpainted; there is not a bush, or garden, or green thing; it just straggles out promiscuously on the boundless brown plains, on the extreme verge of which three toothy peaks are seen. It is utterly slovenly-looking and unornamental, abounds in slouching bar-room-looking characters, and looks a place of low, mean lives. Below the hotel window freight cars are being perpetually shunted, but beyond the railroad tracks are nothing but the brown plains, with their lonely sights—now a solitary horseman at a traveling amble, then a party of Indians in paint and feathers, but civilized up to the point of carrying firearms, mounted on sorry ponies, the bundled-up squaws riding astride on the baggage ponies; then a drove of ridgy-spined, long-horned cattle, which have been several months eating their way from Texas, with their escort of four or five much-spurred horsemen, in peaked hats, blue-hooded coats, and high boots, heavily armed with revolvers and repeating rifles, and riding small wiry horses. A solitary wagon, with a white tilt, drawn by eight oxen, is probably bearing an emigrant and his fortunes to Colorado. On one of the

[2] The discovery of gold in the Black Hills has lately given it a great impetus, and as it is the chief point of departure for the diggings it is increasing in population and importance. (July, 1879)

dreary spaces of the settlement six white-tilted wagons, each with twelve oxen, are standing on their way to a distant part. Everything suggests a beyond.

September 9.

I have found at the post office here a circular letter of recommendation from ex-Governor Hunt, procured by Miss Kingsley's kindness, and another equally valuable one of "authentication" and recommendation from Mr. Bowles, of the *Springfield Republican*, whose name is a household word in all the West. Armed with these, I shall plunge boldly into Colorado. I am suffering from giddiness and nausea produced by the bad smells. A "help" here says that there have been fifty-six deaths from cholera during the last twenty days. Is common humanity lacking, I wonder, in this region of hard greed? Can it not be bought by dollars here, like every other commodity, votes included? Last night I made the acquaintance of a shadowy gentleman from Wisconsin, far gone in consumption, with a spirited wife and young baby. He had been ordered to the Plains as a last resource, but was much worse. Early this morning he crawled to my door, scarcely able to speak from debility and bleeding from the lungs, begging me to go to his wife, who, the doctor said was ill of cholera. The child had been ill all night, and not for love or money could he get any one to do anything for them, not even to go for the medicine. The lady was blue, and in great pain from cramp, and the poor unweaned infant was roaring for the nourishment which had failed. I vainly tried to get hot water and mustard for a poultice, and though I offered a Negro a dollar to go for the medicine, he looked at it superciliously, hummed a tune, and said he must wait for the Pacific train, which was not due for an hour. Equally in vain I hunted through Cheyenne for a feeding bottle. Not a maternal heart softened to the helpless mother and starving child, and my last resource was to dip a piece of sponge in some milk and water, and try to pacify the creature. I applied Rigollot's leaves, went for the medicine, saw the popular host—a bachelor—who mentioned a girl who, after much difficulty, consented to take charge of the baby for two dollars a day and attend to the mother, and having remained till she began to amend, I took the cars for Greeley, a settlement on the Plains, which I had been recommended to make my starting point for the mountains.

FORT COLLINS, *September 10.*

It gave me a strange sensation to embark upon the Plains. Plains, plains everywhere, plains generally level, but elsewhere rolling in long undulations, like the waves of a sea which had fallen asleep. They are covered thinly with buff grass, the withered stalks of flowers, Spanish bayonet, and a small beehive-shaped cactus. One could gallop all over them.

They are peopled with large villages of what are called prairie dogs, because they utter a short, sharp bark, but the dogs are, in reality, marmots. We passed numbers of villages, which are composed of raised circular orifices, about eighteen inches in diameter, with sloping passages leading downwards for five or six feet. Hundreds of these burrows are placed together. On nearly every rim a small furry reddish-buff beast sat on his hind legs, looking, so far as head went, much like a young seal. These creatures were acting as sentinels, and sunning themselves. As we passed, each gave a warning yelp, shook its tail, and, with a ludicrous flourish of its hind legs, dived into its hole. The appearance of hundreds of these creatures, each eighteen inches long, sitting like dogs begging, with their paws down and all turned sunwards, is most grotesque. The Wish-ton-Wish has few enemies, and is a most prolific animal. From its enormous increase and the energy and extent of its burrowing operations, one can fancy that in the course of years the prairies will be seriously injured, as it honeycombs the ground, and renders it unsafe for horses. The burrows seem usually to be shared by owls, and many of the people insist that a rattlesnake is also an inmate, but I hope for the sake of the harmless, cheery little prairie dog, that this unwelcome fellowship is a myth.

After running on a down grade for some time, five distinct ranges of mountains, one above another, a lurid blue against a lurid sky, upheaved themselves above the prairie sea. An American railway car, hot, stuffy and full of chewing, spitting Yankees, was not an ideal way of approaching this range which had early impressed itself upon my imagination. Still, it was truly grand, although it was sixty miles off, and we were looking at it from a platform 5,000 feet in height. As I write I am only twenty-five miles from them, and they are gradually gaining possession of me. I can look at and *feel* nothing else. At five in the afternoon frame houses and green fields began to appear, the cars drew up, and two of my fellow passengers and I got out and carried our own luggage through the deep dust to a small, rough, Western tavern, where with difficuty we were put up for the night. This settlement is called the Greeley Temperance Colony, and was founded lately by an industrious class of emigrants from the East, all total abstainers, and holding advanced political opinions. They bought and fenced 50,000 acres of land, constructed an irrigating canal, which distributes its waters on reasonable terms, have already a population of 3,000, and are the most prosperous and rising colony in Colorado, being altogether free from either laziness or crime. Their rich fields are artificially productive solely; and after seeing regions where Nature gives spontaneously, one is amazed that people should settle here to be dependent on irrigating canals, with the risk of having their crops destroyed by grasshoppers. A clause in the charter of the colony prohibits the introduction, sale, or consumption of intoxicating liquor, and I hear that the men of Greeley carry their crusade against drink even beyond their limits, and have lately sacked three houses open for the sale of drink near their frontier, pouring the whisky upon the ground, so that people don't now like to run the risk of bringing liquor near Greeley, and the temperance influence is spreading over a very large area. As the men have no bar-rooms to sit in, I observed that Greeley was asleep at an hour when other places were beginning their revelries. Nature is niggardly, and living is coarse and rough, the merest necessaries of hardy life being all that can be thought of in this stage of existence.

My first experiences of Colorado travel have been rather severe. At Greeley I got a small upstairs room at first, but gave it up to a married couple with a child, and then had one downstairs no bigger than a cabin, with only a canvas partition. It was very hot, and every place was thick with black flies. The English landlady had just lost her "help," and was in a great fuss, so that I helped her to get supper ready. Its chief features were greasiness and black flies. Twenty men in working clothes fed and went out again, "nobody speaking to nobody." The landlady introduced me to a Vermont settler who lives in the "Foot Hills," who was very kind and took a great deal of trouble to get me a horse. Horses abound, but they are either large American horses, which are only used for draught, or small, active horses, called *broncos,* said to be from a Spanish word, signifying that they can never be broke. They nearly all "buck," and are described as being more "ugly" and treacherous than mules. There is only one horse in Greeley "safe for a woman to ride." I tried an Indian pony by moonlight—such a moonlight—but found he had tender feet. The kitchen was the only sitting room, so I shortly went to bed, to be awoke very soon by crawling creatures apparently in myriads. I struck a light, and found such swarms of bugs that I gathered myself up on the wooden chairs, and dozed uneasily till sunrise. Bugs are a great pest in Colorado. They come out of the earth, infest the wooden walls, and cannot be got rid of by any amount of cleanliness. Many careful housewives take their beds to pieces every week and put carbolic acid on them.

It was a glorious, cool morning, and the great range of the Rocky Mountains looked magnificent. I tried the pony again, but found he would not do for a long journey; and as my Vermont acquaintance offered me a seat in his wagon to Fort Collins, twenty-five miles nearer the Mountains, I threw a few things together and came here with him. We left Greeley at 10, and arrived here at 4:30, staying an hour for food on the way. I liked the first half of the drive; but the fierce, ungoverned, blazing heat of

the sun on the whitish earth for the last half, was terrible
even with my white umbrella, which I have not used since
I left New Zealand; it was sickening. Then the eyes have
never anything green to rest upon, except in the river bot-
toms, where there is green hay grass. We followed mostly
the course of the River Cache-a-la-Poudre, which rises in
the Mountains, and after supplying Greeley with irrigation, falls into the Platte, which is an affluent of the Mis-
souri. When once beyond the scattered houses and great
ring fence of the vigorous Greeley colonists, we were on
the boundless prairie. Now and then horsemen passed us,
and we met three wagons with white tilts. Except where
the prairie dogs have honeycombed the ground, you can
drive almost anywhere, and the passage of a few wagons
over the same track makes a road. We forded the river,
whose course is marked the whole way by a fringe of small
cotton-woods and aspens, and traveled hour after hour
with nothing to see except some dog towns, with their
quaint little sentinels; but the view in front was glorious.
The Alps, from the Lombard Plains, are the finest mountain panorama I ever saw, but not equal to this; for not
only do five high-peaked giants, each nearly the height of
Mont Blanc, lift their dazzling summits above the lower
ranges, but the expanse of mountains is so vast, and the
whole lie in a transparent medium of the richest blue, not
haze—something peculiar to the region. The lack of foreground is a great artistic fault, and the absence of green-
ery is melancholy, and makes me recall sadly the entrancing detail of the Hawaiian Islands. Once only, the second
time we forded the river, the cotton-woods formed a
foreground, and then the loveliness was heavenly. We
stopped at a log house and got a rough dinner of beef and

33

potatoes, and I was amused at the five men who shared it with us for apologizing to me for being without their coats, as if coats would not be an enormity on the Plains.

It is the election day for the Territory, and men were galloping over the prairie to register their votes. The three in the wagon talked politics the whole time. They spoke openly and shamelessly of the prices given for votes; and apparently there was not a politician on either side who was not accused of degrading corruption. We saw a convoy of 5,000 head of Texas cattle traveling from southern Texas to Iowa. They had been nine months on the way! They were under the charge of twenty mounted *vacheros*, heavily armed, and a light wagon accompanied them, full of extra rifles and ammunition, not unnecessary, for the Indians are raiding in all directions, maddened by the reckless and useless slaughter of the buffalo, which is their chief subsistence. On the Plains are herds of wild horses, buffalo, deer, and antelope; and in the Mountains, bears, wolves, deer, elk, mountain lions, bison, and mountain sheep. You see a rifle in every wagon, as people always hope to fall in with game.

By the time we reached Fort Collins I was sick and dizzy with the heat of the sun, and not disposed to be pleased with a most unpleasing place. It was a military post, but at present consists of a few frame houses put down recently on the bare and burning plain. The settlers have "great expectations," but of what? The Mountains look hardly nearer than from Greeley; one only realizes their vicinity by the loss of their higher peaks. This house is freer from bugs than the one at Greeley, but full of flies. These new settlements are altogether revolting, entirely utilitarian, given up to talk of dollars as well as to making them, with

34

coarse speech, coarse food, coarse everything, nothing wherewith to satisfy the higher cravings if they exist, nothing on which the eye can rest with pleasure, The lower floor of this inn swarms with locusts in addition to thousands of black flies. The latter cover the ground and rise buzzing from it as you walk.

I. L. B.

Letter IV

✳

✤✿➤✤✿➤✤✿➤✤✿➤✤✿➤✤✿➤✤✿➤✤✿➤✤✿➤✤✿➤✤✿➤✤✿➤✤✿➤

A PLAGUE OF FLIES—A MELANCHOLY CHARIOTEER—THE
FOOT HILLS—A MOUNTAIN BOARDING-HOUSE—A DULL
LIFE—"BEING AGREEABLE"—CLIMATE OF COLORADO—
Soroche AND SNAKES.

✤✿➤✤✿➤✤✿➤✤✿➤✤✿➤✤✿➤✤✿➤✤✿➤✤✿➤✤✿➤✤✿➤✤✿➤✤✿➤

CANYON, *September 12.*

I was actually so dull and tired that I deliberately slept
away the afternoon in order to forget the heat and flies.
Thirty men in working clothes, silent and sad looking,
came in to supper. The beef was tough and greasy, the
butter had turned to oil, and beef and butter were black
with living, drowned, and half-drowned flies. The greasy
table-cloth was black also with flies, and I did not wonder
that the guests looked melancholy and quickly escaped.
I failed to get a horse, but was strongly recommended to
come here and board with a settler, who, they said, had a
saw-mill and took boarders. The person who recommended it so strongly gave me a note of introduction,
and told me that it was in a grand part of the mountains,
where many people had been camping out all the summer
for the benefit of their health. The idea of a boarding-
house, as I know them in America, was rather formidable
in the present state of my wardrobe, and I decided on
bringing my carpet-bag, as well as my pack, lest I should
be rejected for my bad clothes.

Early the next morning I left in a buggy drawn by light

broncos and driven by a profoundly melancholy young man. He had never been to the canyon; there was no road. We met nobody, saw nothing except antelope in the distance, and he became more melancholy and lost his way, driving hither and thither for about twenty miles till we came upon an old trail which eventually brought us to a fertile "bottom," where hay and barley were being harvested, and five or six frame houses looked cheerful. I had been recommended to two of these, which professed to take in strangers, but one was full of reapers, and in the other a child was dead. So I took the buggy on, glad to leave the glaring, prosaic settlement behind. There was a most curious loneliness about the journey up to that time. Except for the huge barrier to the right, the boundless prairies were everywhere, and it was like being at sea without a compass. The wheels made neither sound nor indentation as we drove over the short, dry grass, and there was no cheerful clatter of horses' hoofs. The sky was cloudy and the air hot and still. In one place we passed the carcass of a mule, and a number of vultures soared up from it, to descend again immediately. Skeletons and bones of animals were often to be seen. A range of low, grassy hills, called the Foot Hills, rose from the plain, featureless and monotonous, except where streams, fed by the snows of the higher regions, had cut their way through them. Confessedly bewildered, and more melancholy than ever, the driver turned up one of the wildest of these entrances, and in another hour the Foot Hills lay between us and the prairie sea, and a higher and broken range, with pitch pines of average size, was revealed behind them. These Foot Hills, which swell up uninterestingly from the plains on their eastern side, on their western have the appearance of having broken off from the next range, and the break is abrupt, and takes the form of walls and terraces of rock of the most brilliant color, weathered and stained by ores, and, even under the grey sky, dazzling to the eyes. The driver thought he had understood the directions given, but he was stupid, and once we lost some miles by arriving at a river too rough and deep to be forded, and again we were brought up by an impassable canyon. He grew frightened about his horses, and said no money would ever tempt him into the mountains again; but average intelligence would have made it all easy.

The solitude was becoming somber, when, after driving for nine hours, and traveling at the least forty-five miles, without any sign of fatigue on the part of the *broncos*, we came to a stream, by the side of which we drove along a definite track, till we came to a sort of tri-partite valley, with a majestic crooked canyon 2,000 feet deep opening upon it. A rushing stream roared through it, and the Rocky Mountains, with pines scattered over them, came down upon it. A little farther, and the canyon became utterly inaccessible. This was exciting; here was an inner world. A rough and shaky bridge, made of the outsides of pines laid upon some unsecured logs, crossed the river. The *broncos* stopped and smelt it, not liking it, but some encouraging speech induced them to go over. On the other side was a log cabin, partially ruinous, and the very rudest I ever saw, its roof of plastered mud being broken into large holes. It stood close to the water among some cotton-wood trees. A little higher there was a very primitive saw-mill, also out of repair, with some logs lying about. An emigrant wagon and a forlorn tent, with a camp-fire and a pot, were in the foreground, but there was no trace of the boarding-house, of which I stood a little in dread. The driver went for further directions to the log cabin, and returned with a grim smile deepening the melancholy of his face to say it was Mr. Chalmers', but there was no accommodation for such as him, much less for me! This was truly "a sell." I got down and found a single room of the rudest kind, with the wall at one end partially broken down, holes in the roof, holes for windows, and no furniture but two chairs and two unplaned wooden shelves, with some sacks of straw upon them for beds. There was an adjacent cabin room, with a stove, benches, and table, where they cooked and ate, but this was all. A hard, sad-looking woman looked at me measuringly. She said that they sold milk and butter to parties who camped in the canyon, that they had never had any boarders but two asthmatic old ladies, but they would take me for five dollars per week if I "would make myself agreeable." The horses had to be fed, and I sat down on a box, had some dried beef and milk, and considered the matter. If I went back to Fort Collins, I thought I was farther from a mountain life, and had no choice but Denver, a place from which I shrank, or to take the cars for New York. Here the life was rough, rougher than any I had ever seen, and the people repelled me by their faces and manners; but if I could rough it for a few days, I might, I thought, get over canyons and all other difficulties into Estes Park, which has become the goal of my journey and hopes. So I decided to remain.

September 16.

Five days here, and I am no nearer Estes Park. How the days pass I know not; I am weary of the limitations of this existence. This is "a life in which nothing happens." When the buggy disappeared, I felt as if I had cut the bridge behind me. I sat down and knitted for some time—my usual resource under discouraging circumstances. I really did not know how I should get on. There was no table, no bed, no basin, no towel, no glass, no window, no fastening on the door. The roof was in holes, the logs were un-chinked, and one end of the cabin was partially removed! Life was reduced to its simplest elements. I went out; the family all had something to do, and took no notice of me. I went back, and then an awkward girl of sixteen, with uncombed hair, and a painful repulsiveness of face and air, sat on a log for half an hour and stared at me. I tried to draw her into talk, but she twirled her fingers and replied snappishly in monosyllables. Could I by any effort "make myself agreeable"? I wondered. The day went on. I put on my Hawaiian dress, rolling up the sleeves to the elbows in an "agreeable" fashion. Towards evening the family returned to feed, and pushed some dried beef and milk in at the door. They all slept under the trees, and before dark carried the sacks of straw out for their bedding. I followed their example that night, or rather watched Charles's Wain while they slept, but since then have slept on blankets on the floor under the roof. They have neither lamp nor candle, so if I want to do anything after dark I have to do it by the unsteady light of pine knots. As the nights are cold, and free from bugs, and I do a good deal of manual labor, I sleep well. At dusk I make my bed on the floor, and draw a bucket of ice-cold water from the river; the family go to sleep under the trees, and I pile logs on the fire sufficient to burn half the night, for I assure you the solitude is *eerie* enough. There are unaccountable noises, (wolves), rummagings under the floor, queer cries, and stealthy sounds of I know not what. One night a beast (fox or skunk) rushed in at the open end of the cabin, and fled through the window, almost brushing my face, and on another, the head and three or four inches of the body of a snake were protruded through a chink of the floor close to me, to my extreme disgust. My mirror is the polished inside of my watchcase. At sunrise Mrs. Chalmers comes in—if coming into a nearly open shed can be called *in*— and makes a fire, because she thinks me too stupid to do it, and mine is the family room; and by seven I am dressed, have folded the blankets, and swept the floor, and then she puts some milk and bread or stirabout on a box by the door. After breakfast I draw more water, and wash one or two garments daily, taking care that there are no witnesses of my inexperience. Yesterday a calf sucked one into hopeless rags. The rest of the day I spend in mending, knitting, writing to you, and the various odds and ends which arise when one has to do all for oneself. At twelve and six some food is put on the box by the door, and at dusk we make up our beds. A distressed emigrant woman has just given birth to a child in a temporary shanty by the river, and I go to help her each day.

I have made the acquaintance of all the careworn, struggling settlers within a walk. All have come for health, and most have found or are finding it, even if they have not better shelter than a wagon tilt or a blanket on sticks laid across four poles. The climate of Colorado is considered the finest in North America, and consumptives, asthmatics, dyspeptics, and sufferers from nervous diseases, are here in hundreds and thousands, either trying the "camp cure" for three or four months, or settling here permanently.

People can safely sleep out of doors for six months of the year. The plains are from 4,000 to 6,000 feet high, and some of the settled "parks," or mountain valleys, are from 8,000 to 10,000. The air, besides being much rarefied, is very dry. The rainfall is far below the average, dews are rare, and fogs nearly unknown. The sunshine is bright and almost constant, and three-fourths of the days are cloudless. The milk, beef, and bread are good. The climate is neither so hot in summer nor so cold in winter as that of the States, and when the days are hot the nights are cool. Snow rarely lies on the lower ranges, and horses and cattle don't require to be either fed or housed during the winter. Of course the rarefied air quickens respiration. All this is from hearsay.[1] I am not under favorable circumstances, either for mind or body, and at present I feel a singular lassitude and difficulty in taking exercise, but this is said to be the milder form of the affection known on higher altitudes as *soroche*, or "mountain sickness," and is only temporary. I am forming a plan for getting farther into the mountains, and hope that my next letter will be more lively. I killed a rattlesnake this morning close to the cabin, and have taken its rattle, which has eleven joints. My life is embittered by the abundance of these reptiles—rattlesnakes and moccasin snakes, both deadly, carpet snakes and "green racers," reputed dangerous, water snakes, tree snakes, and mouse snakes, harmless but abominable. Seven rattlesnakes have been killed just outside the cabin since

[1] The curative effect of the climate of Colorado can hardly be exaggerated. In traveling extensively through the Territory afterwards I found that nine out of every ten settlers were cured invalids. Statistics and medical works on the climate of the State (as it now is) represent Colorado as the most remarkable sanatorium in the world.

I came. A snake, three feet long, was coiled under the pillow of the sick woman. I see snakes in all withered twigs, and am ready to flee at "the sound of a shaken leaf." And besides snakes, the earth and air are alive and noisy with forms of insect life, large and small, stinging, humming, buzzing, striking, rasping, devouring!

I. L. B.

Letter V

⊹⊕⊹✻⊹⊕⊹✻⊹⊕⊹✻⊹⊕⊹✻⊹⊕⊹✻⊹⊕⊹✻⊹⊕⊹✻⊹⊕⊹✻⊹⊕⊹✻⊹⊕⊹✻⊹⊕

A DATELESS DAY—"THOSE HANDS OF YOURS"—A PURI-
TAN—PERSEVERING SHIFTLESSNESS—THE HOUSE-MOTHER
—FAMILY WORSHIP—A GRIM SUNDAY—A "THICK-
SKULLED ENGLISHMAN"—A MORNING CALL—ANOTHER
ATMOSPHERE—THE GREAT LONE LAND—"ILL FOUND"
—A LOG CAMP—BAD FOOTING FOR HORSES—ACCIDENTS—
DISAPPOINTMENT.

⊹⊕⊹✻⊹⊕⊹✻⊹⊕⊹✻⊹⊕⊹✻⊹⊕⊹✻⊹⊕⊹✻⊹⊕⊹✻⊹⊕⊹✻⊹⊕⊹✻⊹⊕⊹✻⊹⊕

CANYON, *September*.

The absence of a date shows my predicament. *They* have
no newspaper; *I* have no almanack; the father is away for
the day, and none of the others can help me, and they look
contemptuously upon my desire for information on the
subject. The monotony will come to an end to-morrow,
for Chalmers offers to be my guide over the mountains to
Estes Park, and has persuaded his wife "for once to go for
a frolic"; and with much reluctance, many growls at the
waste of time, and many apprehensions of danger and loss,
she has consented to accompany him. My life has grown
less dull from their having become more interesting to me,
and as I have "made myself agreeable," we are on fairly
friendly terms. My first move in the direction of fraterniz-
ing was, however, snubbed. A few days ago, having finished my own work, I offered to wash up the plates, but
Mrs. C., with a look which conveyed more than words, a
curl of her nose, and a sneer in her twang, said "Guess

you'll make more work nor you'll do. Those hands of yours" (very brown and coarse they were) "ain't no good; never done nothing, I guess." Then to her awkward daughter: "This woman says she'll wash up! Ha! ha! look at her arms and hands!" This was the nearest approach to a laugh I have heard, and have never seen even a tendency towards a smile. Since then I have risen in their estimation by improvizing a lamp—Hawaiian fashion—by putting a wisp of rag into a tin of fat. They have actually condescended to sit up till the stars come out since. Another advance was made by means of the shell-pattern quilt I am knitting for you. There has been a tendency towards approving of it, and a few days since the girl snatched it out of my hand, saying, "I want this," and apparently took it to the camp. This has resulted in my having a knitting class, with the woman, her married daughter, and a woman from the camp, as pupils. Then I have gained ground with the man by being able to catch and saddle a horse. I am often reminded of my favorite couplet, —

> *Beware of desperate steps; the darkest day,*
> *Live till to-morrow, will have passed away.*

But oh! what a hard, narrow life it is with which I am now in contact! A narrow and unattractive religion, which I believe still to be genuine, and an intense but narrow patriotism, are the only higher influences. Chalmers came from Illinois nine years ago, pronounced by the doctors to be far gone in consumption, and in two years he was strong. They are a queer family; somewhere in the remote Highlands I have seen such another. Its head is tall, gaunt, lean, and ragged, and has lost one eye. On an English road one would think him a starving or a dangerous beggar.

He is slightly intelligent, very opinionated, and wishes to be thought well informed, which he is not. He belongs to the straitest sect of Reformed Presbyterians ("Psalm-singers"), but exaggerates anything of bigotry and intolerance which may characterize them, and rejoices in truly merciless fashion over the excision of the philanthropic Mr. Stuart, of Philadelphia, for worshipping with congregations which sing hymns. His great boast is that his ancestors were Scottish Covenanters. He considers himself a profound theologian, and by the pine logs at night discourses to me on the mysteries of the eternal counsels and the divine decrees. Colorado, with its progress and its future, is also a constant theme. He hates England with a bitter, personal hatred, and regards any allusions which I make to the progress of Victoria as a personal insult. He trusts to live to see the downfall of the British monarchy and the disintegration of the empire. He is very fond of talking, and asks me a great deal about my travels, but if I speak favorably of the climate or resources of any other country, he regards it as a slur on Colorado.

They have one hundred and sixty acres of land, a "Squatter's claim," and an invaluable water power. He is a lumberer, and has a saw-mill of a very primitive kind. I notice that every day something goes wrong with it, and this is the case throughout. If he wants to haul timber down, one or other of the oxen cannot be found; or if the timber is actually under way, a wheel or a part of the harness gives way, and the whole affair is at a standstill for days. The cabin is hardly a shelter, but is allowed to remain in ruins because the foundation of a frame house was once a dug. A horse is always sure to be lame for want of a shoe nail, or a saddle to be useless from a broken buckle, and the wagon and harness are a marvel of temporary shifts, patchings, and insecure linkings with strands of rope. Nothing is ever ready or whole when it is wanted. Yet Chalmers is a frugal, sober, hard-working man, and he, his eldest son, and a "hired man" "Rise early," "going forth to their work and labor till the evening;" and if they do not "late take rest," they truly "eat the bread of carefulness." It is hardly surprising that nine years of persevering shiftlessness should have resulted in nothing but the ability to procure the bare necessaries of life.

Of Mrs. C. I can say less. She looks like one of the English poor women of our childhood—lean, clean, toothless, and speaks, like some of them, in a piping, discontented voice, which seems to convey a personal reproach. All her waking hours are spent in a large sun-bonnet. She is never idle for one minute, is severe and hard, and despises everything but work. I think she suffers from her husband's shiftlessness. She always speaks of me as "This" or "that woman." The family consists of a grown-up son, a shiftless, melancholy-looking youth, who possibly pines for a wider life; a girl of sixteen, a sour, repellent-looking creature, with as much manners as a pig; and three hard, unchild-like younger children. By the whole family all courtesy and gentleness of act or speech seem regarded as "works of the flesh," if not of "the devil." They knock over all one's things without apologizing or picking them up, and when I thank them for anything they look grimly amazed. I feel that they think it sinful that I do not work as hard as they do. I wish I could show them "a more excellent way." This hard greed, and the exclusive pursuit of gain, with the indifference to all which does not aid in its acquisition, are eating up family love and life throughout the West. I write this reluctantly, and after a total experience of nearly two years in the United States. They seem to have no "Sunday clothes," and few of any kind. The sewing machine, like most other things, is out of order. One comb serves the whole family. Mrs. C. is cleanly in her person and dress, and the food, though poor, is clean. Work, work, work, is their day and their life. They are thoroughly ungenial, and have that air of suspicion in speaking of every one which is not unusual in the land of their ancestors. Thomas Chalmers is the man's ecclesiastical hero, in spite of his own severe Puritanism. Their live stock consists of two wretched horses, a fairly good *bronco* mare, a mule, four badly-bred cows, four gaunt and famished-looking oxen, some swine of singularly active habits, and plenty of poultry. The old saddles are tied on with twine; one side of the bridle is a worn-out strap and the other a rope. They wear boots, but never two of one pair, and never blacked, of course, but no stockings. They think it quite effeminate to sleep under a roof, except during the severest months of the year. There is a married daughter across the river, just the same hard, loveless, moral, hard-working being as her mother. Each morning, soon after seven, when I have swept the cabin, the family come in for "worship." Chalmers "wales" a psalm, in every sense of the word wail, to the most doleful of dismal tunes; they read a chapter round, and he prays. If his prayer has something of the tone of the imprecatory psalms, he has high authority in his favor; and if there be a tinge of the Pharisaic thanksgiving, it is hardly surprising that he is grateful that he is not as other men are when he contemplates the general godlessness of the region.

Sunday was a dreadful day. The family kept the Commandment literally, and did no work. Worship was conducted twice, and was rather longer than usual. Chalmers does not allow of any books in his house but theological works, and two or three volumes of dull travels, so the mother and children slept nearly all day. The man attempted to read a well-worn copy of *Boston's Fourfold State*, but shortly fell asleep, and they only woke up for their meals. Friday and Saturday had been passably cool, with frosty nights, but on Saturday night it changed, and I have not felt anything like the heat of Sunday since I left New Zealand, though the mercury was not higher than $91°$. It was sickening, scorching, melting, unbearable, from the mere power of the sun's rays. It was an awful day, and seemed as if it would never come to an end. The cabin, with its mud roof under the shade of the trees, gave a little shelter, but it was occupied by the family, and I longed for solitude. I took the *Imitation of Christ*, and strolled up the canyon among the withered, crackling leaves, in much dread of snakes, and lay down on a rough table which some passing emigrant had left, and soon fell asleep. When I awoke it was only noon. The sun looked wicked as it blazed like a white magnesium light. A large tree-snake (quite harmless) hung from the pine under which I had taken shelter, and looked as if it were going to drop upon me. I was covered with black flies. The air was full of a busy, noisy din of insects, and snakes, locusts, wasps, flies, and grasshoppers were all rioting in the torrid heat. Would the sublime philosophy of Thomas à Kempis, I wondered, have given way under this? All day I seemed to hear in mockery the clear laugh of the Hilo streams, and the drip of Knoa showers, and to see as in a mirage the

49

perpetual green of windward Hawaii. I was driven back to the cabin in the late afternoon, and in the evening listened for two hours to abuse of my own country, and to sweeping condemnations of all religionists outside of the brotherhood of "Psalm-singers." It is jarring and painful, yet I would say of Chalmers, as Dr. Holland says of another: —

> *If ever I shall reach the home in heaven,*
> *For whose dear rest I humbly hope and pray,*
> *In the great company of the forgiven*
> *I shall be sure to meet old Daniel Gray.*

The night came without coolness, but at daylight on Monday morning a fire was pleasant. You will now have some idea of my surroundings. It is a moral, hard, unloving, unlovely, unrelieved, unbeautified, grinding life. These people live in a discomfort and lack of ease and refinement which seems only possible to people of British stock. A "foreigner" fills his cabin with ingenuities and elegancies, and a Hawaiian or South Sea Islander makes his grass house both pretty and tasteful. Add to my surroundings a mighty canyon, impassable both above and below, and walls of mountains with an opening some miles off to the vast prairie sea.[1]

An English physician is settled about half a mile from here over a hill. He is spoken of as holding "very extreme opinions." Chalmers rails at him for being "a thick-skulled Englishman," for being "fine, polished," etc. To say a man

[1] I have not curtailed this description of the roughness of a Colorado settler's life, for, with the exceptions of the disrepair and the Puritanism, it is a type of the hard, unornamented existence with which I came almost universally in contact during my subsequent residence in the Territory.

is "polished" here is to give him a very bad name. He
accuses him also of holding views subversive of all morality. In spite of all this, I thought he might possess a map,
and I induced Mrs. C. to walk over with me. She intended
it as a formal morning call, but she wore the inevitable
sun-bonnet, and had her dress tied up as when washing.
It was not till I reached the gate that I remembered that
I was in my Hawaiian riding dress, and that I still wore
the spurs with which I had been trying a horse in the
morning! The house was in a grass valley which opened
from the tremendous canyon through which the river had
cut its way. The Foot Hills, with their terraces of flaming
red rock, were glowing in the sunset, and a pure green sky
arched tenderly over a soft evening scene. Used to the
meanness and baldness of settlers' dwellings, I was de-
lighted to see that in this instance the usual log cabin was
only the lower floor of a small house, which bore a delightful resemblance to a Swiss châlet. It stood in a vegetable
garden fertilized by an irrigating ditch, outside of which
were a barn and cowshed. A young Swiss girl was bringing the cows slowly home from the hill, an Englishwoman
in a clean print dress stood by the fence holding a baby,
and a fine-looking Englishman in a striped Garibaldi shirt,
and trousers of the same tucked into high boots, was shell-
ing corn. As soon as Mrs. Hughes spoke I felt she was
truly a lady; and oh! how refreshing her refined, courteous, graceful English manner was, as she invited us into
the house! The entrance was low, through a log porch
festooned and almost concealed by a "wild cucumber."
Inside, though plain and poor, the room looked a home,
not like a squatter's cabin. An old tin was completely covered by a graceful clematis mixed with streamers of Vir-

51

ginia creeper, and white muslin curtains, and above all two shelves of admirably-chosen books, gave the room almost an air of elegance. Why do I write almost? It was an oasis. It was barely three weeks since I had left "the communion of educated men," and the first tones of the voices of my host and hostess made me feel as if I had been out of it for a year. Mrs. C. stayed an hour and a half, and then went home to the cows, when we launched upon a sea of congenial talk. They said they had not seen an educated lady for two years, and pressed me to go and visit them. I rode home on Dr. Hughes's horse after dark, to find neither fire nor light in the cabin. Mrs. C. had gone back saying, "Those English talked just like savages, I couldn't understand a word they said."

I made a fire, and extemporized a light with some fat and a wick of rag, and Chalmers came in to discuss my visit and to ask me a question concerning a matter which had roused the latent curiosity of the whole family. I had told him, he said, that I knew no one hereabouts, but "his woman" told him that Dr. H. and I spoke constantly of a Mrs. Grundy, whom we both knew and disliked, and who was settled, as we said, not far off! He had never heard of her, he said, and he was the pioneer settler of the canyon, and there was a man up here from Longmount who said he was sure there was not a Mrs. Grundy in the district, unless it was a woman who went by two names! The wife and family had then come in, and I felt completely nonplussed. I longed to tell Chalmers that it was he and such as he, there or anywhere, with narrow hearts, bitter tongues, and harsh judgments, who were the true "Mrs. Grundys," dwarfing individuality, checking lawful freedom of speech, and making men "offenders for a word," but I forebore. How I extricated myself from the difficulty, deponent sayeth not. The rest of the evening has been spent in preparing to cross the mountains. Chalmers says he knows the way well, and that we shall sleep tomorrow at the foot of Long's Peak. Mrs. Chalmers repents of having consented, and conjures up doleful visions of what the family will come to when left headless, and of disasters among the cows and hens. I could tell her that the eldest son and the "hired man" have plotted to close the saw-mill and go on a hunting and fishing expedition, that the cows will stray, and that the individual spoken respectfully of as "Mr. Skunk" will make havoc in the hen-house.

NAMELESS REGION, ROCKY MOUNTAINS, *September*.

This is indeed far removed. It seems farther away from you than any place I have been to yet, except the frozen top of the volcano of Mauna Loa. It is so little profaned by man that if one were compelled to live here in solitude one might truly say of the bears, deer, and elk which abound, "Their tameness is shocking to me." It is the world of "big game." Just now a heavy-headed elk, with much-branched horns fully three feet long, stood and looked at me, and then quietly trotted away. He was so near that I heard the grass, crisp with hoar frost, crackle under his feet. Bears stripped the cherry bushes within a few yards of us last night. Now two lovely blue birds, with crests on their heads, are picking about within a stone's-throw. This is "The Great Lone Land," until lately the hunting ground of the Indians, and not yet settled or traversed, or likely to be so, owing to the want of water. A solitary hunter has built a log cabin up here, which he occupies for a few weeks for the purpose of elk-hunting, but all the region is unsurveyed, and mostly un-explored. It is 7 A.M. The sun has not yet risen high enough to melt the hoar frost, and the air is clear, bright, and cold. The stillness is profound. I hear nothing but the far-off mysterious roaring of a river in a deep canyon, which we spent two hours last night in trying to find. The horses are lost, and if I were disposed to retort upon my companions the term they invariably apply to me, I should now write, with bitter emphasis, "*that* man" and "*that* woman" have gone in search of them.

The scenery up here is glorious, combining sublimity with beauty, and in the elastic air fatigue has dropped off from me. This is no region for tourists and women, only for a few elk and bear hunters at times, and its unprofaned freshness gives me new life. I cannot by any words give you an idea of scenery so different from any that you or I have ever seen. This is an upland valley of grass and flowers, of glades and sloping lawns, and cherry-fringed beds of dry streams, and clumps of pines artistically placed, and mountain sides densely pine clad, the pines breaking into fringes as they come down upon the "park," and the mountains breaking into pinnacles of bold grey rock as they pierce the blue of the sky. A single dell of bright green grass, on which dwarf clumps of the scarlet poison oak look like beds of geraniums, slopes towards the west, as if it must lead to the river which we seek. Deep, vast canyons, all trending westwards, lie in purple gloom. Pine-clad ranges, rising into the blasted top of Storm Peak, all run westwards too, and all the beauty and glory are but the frame out of which rises—heaven-piercing, pure in its pearly luster, as glorious a mountain as the sun tinges red in either hemisphere—the splintered, pinnacled, lonely, ghastly, imposing, double-peaked summit of Long's Peak, the Mont Blanc of Northern Colorado.[2]

This is a view to which nothing needs to be added. This is truly the "lodge in some vast wilderness" for which one often sighs when in the midst of "a bustle at once sordid and trivial." In spite of Dr. Johnson, these "monstrous protuberances" do "inflame the imagination and elevate the understanding." This scenery satisfies my soul. Now, the Rocky Mountains realize—nay, exceed—the dream of my childhood. It is magnificent, and the air is life giving. I should like to spend some time in these higher regions, but I know that this will turn out an abortive expedition, owing to the stupidity and pigheadedness of Chalmers.

There is a most romantic place called Estes Park, at a height of 7,500 feet, which can be reached by going down to the plains and then striking up the St. Vrain Canyon, but this is a distance of fifty-five miles, and as Chalmers was confident that he could take me over the mountains, a distance, as he supposed, of about twenty miles, we left at mid-day yesterday, with the fervent hope, on my part, that I might not return. Mrs. C. was busy the whole of Tuesday in preparing what she called "grub," which, together with "plenty of bedding," was to be carried on a pack mule; but when we started I was disgusted to find that Chalmers was on what should have been the pack animal, and that two thickly-quilted cotton "spreads" had

[2] Gray's Peak and Pike's Peak have their partisans, but after seeing them all under favorable aspects, Long's Peak stands in my memory as it does in that vast congeries of mountains, alone in imperial grandeur.

been disposed of under my saddle, making it broad, high, and uncomfortable. Any human being must have laughed to see an expedition start so grotesquely "ill found." I had a very old iron-grey horse, whose lower lip hung down feebly, showing his few teeth, while his fore-legs stuck out forwards, and matter ran from both his nearly-blind eyes. It is kindness to bring him up to abundant pasture. My saddle is an old McLellan cavalry saddle, with a battered brass peak, and the bridle is a rotten leather strap on one side and a strand of rope on the other. The cotton quilts covered the Rosinante from mane to tail. Mrs. C. wore an old print skirt, an old short-gown, a print apron, and a sun-bonnet, with the flap coming down to her waist, and looked as careworn and clean as she always does. The inside horn of her saddle was broken; to the outside one hung a saucepan and a bundle of clothes. The one girth was nearly at the breaking point when we started.

My pack, with my well-worn umbrella upon it, was behind my saddle. I wore my Hawaiian riding dress, with a handkerchief tied over my face and the sun-cover of my umbrella folded and tied over my hat, for the sun was very fierce. The queerest figure of all was the would-be guide. With his one eye, his gaunt, lean form, and his torn clothes, he looked more like a strolling tinker than the honest worthy settler that he is. He bestrode rather than rode a gaunt mule, whose tail hair had all been shaven off, except a turf for a tassel at the end. Two flour bags which leaked were tied on behind the saddle, two quilts were under it, and my canvas bag, a battered canteen, a frying pan, and two lariats hung from the horn. On one foot C. wore an old high boot, into which his trouser was tucked, and on the other an old brogue, through which his toes protruded.

56

We had an ascent of four hours through a ravine which gradually opened out upon this beautiful "park," but we rode through it for some miles before the view burst upon us. The vastness of this range, like astronomical distances, can hardly be conceived of. At this place, I suppose, it is not less than 250 miles wide, and with hardly a break in its continuity, it stretches almost from the Arctic Circle to the Straits of Magellan. From the top of Long's Peak, within a short distance, twenty-two summits, each above 12,000 feet in height, are visible, and the Snowy Range, the backbone or "divide" of the continent, is seen snaking distinctly through the wilderness of ranges, with its waters starting for either ocean. From the first ridge we crossed after leaving Canyon we had a singular view of range beyond range cleft by deep canyons, and abounding in elliptical valleys, richly grassed. The slopes of all the hills, as far as one could see, were waving with fine grass ready for the scythe, but the food of wild animals only. All these ridges are heavily timbered with pitch pines, and where they come down on the grassy slopes they look as if the trees had been arranged by a landscape gardener. Far off, through an opening in a canyon, we saw the prairie simulating the ocean. Far off, through an opening in another direction, was the glistening outline of the Snowy Range. But still, till we reached this place, it was monotonous, though grand as a whole: a grey-green or buff-grey, with outbreaks of brilliantly-colored rock, only varied by the black-green of pines, which are not the stately pyramidal pines of the Sierra Nevada, but much resemble the natural Scotch fir. Not many miles from us is North Park, a great tract of land said to be rich in gold, but those who have gone to "prospect" have seldom returned, the region being

57

the home of tribes of Indians who live in perpetual hostility to the whites and to each other.

At this great height, and most artistically situated, we came upon a rude log camp tenanted in winter by an elk hunter, but now deserted. Chalmers without any scruple picked the padlock; we lighted a fire, made some tea, and fried some bacon, and after a good meal mounted again and started for Estes Park. For four weary hours we searched hither and thither along every indentation of the ground which might be supposed to slope towards the Big Thompson River, which we knew had to be forded. Still, as the quest grew more tedious, Long's Peak stood before us as a landmark in purple glory; and still at his feet lay a hollow filled with deep blue atmosphere, where I knew that Estes Park must lie, and still between us and it lay never-lessening miles of inaccessibility, and the sun was ever westering, and the shadows ever lengthening, and Chalmers, who had started confident, bumptious, blatant, was ever becoming more bewildered, and his wife's thin voice more piping and discontented, and my stumbling horse more insecure, and I more determined (as I am at this moment) that somehow or other I would reach that blue hollow, and even stand on Long's Peak where the snow was glittering. Affairs were becoming serious, and Chalmers's incompetence a source of real peril, when, after an exploring expedition, he returned more bumptious than ever, saying he knew it would be all right, he had found a trail, and we could get across the river by dark, and camp out for the night. So he led us into a steep, deep, rough ravine, where we had to dismount, for trees were lying across it everywhere, and there was almost no footing on the great slabs of shelving rock. Yet there was a trail, tolerably well worn, and the branches and twigs near the ground were well broken back. Ah! it was a wild place. My horse fell first, rolling over twice, and breaking off a part of the saddle, in his second roll knocking me over a shelf of three feet of descent. Then Mrs. C.'s horse and the mule fell on the top of each other, and on recovering themselves bit each other savagely. The ravine became a wild gulch, the dry bed of some awful torrent; there were huge shelves of rock, great overhanging walls of rock, great prostrate trees, cedar spikes and cacti to wound the feet, and then a precipice fully 500 feet deep! The trail was a trail made by bears in search of bear cherries, which abounded!

It was getting dusk as we had to struggle up the rough gulch we had so fatuously descended. The horses fell several times; I could hardly get mine up at all, though I helped him as much as I could; I was cut and bruised, scratched and torn. A spine of a cactus penetrated my foot, and some vicious thing cut the back of my neck. Poor Mrs. C. was much bruised, and I pitied her, for she got no fun out of it as I did. It was an awful climb. When we got out of the gulch, C. was so confused that he took the wrong direction, and after an hour of vague wandering was only recalled to the right one by my pertinacious assertions acting on his weak brain. I was inclined to be angry with the incompetent braggart, who had boasted that he could take us to Estes Park "blindfold"; but I was sorry for him too, so said nothing, even though I had to walk during these meanderings to save my tired horse. When at last, at dark, we reached the open, there was a snow flurry, with violent gusts of wind, and the shelter of the camp, dark and cold as it was, was desirable. We had no food, but made a fire. I lay down on some dry grass, with my inverted saddle for a pillow, and slept soundly, till I was awoke by the cold of an intense frost and the pain of my many cuts and bruises. Chalmers promised that we should make a fresh start at six, so I woke him up at five, and here I am alone at half-past eight! I said to him many times that unless he hobbled or picketed the horses, we should lose them. "Oh," he said "they'll be all right." In truth he had no picketing pins. Now, the animals are merrily trotting homewards. I saw them two miles off an hour ago with him after them. His wife, who is also after them, goaded to desperation, said, "He's the most ignorant, careless, good-for-nothing man I ever saw," upon which I dwelt upon his being well meaning. There is a sort of well here, but our "afternoon tea" and watering the horses drained it, so we have had nothing to drink since yesterday, for the canteen, which started without a cork, lost all its contents when the mule fell. I have made a monstrous fire, but thirst and impatience are hard to bear, and preventible misfortunes are always irksome. I have found the stomach of a bear with fully a pint of cherrystones in it, and have spent an hour in getting the kernels; and lo! now, at half-past nine, I see the culprit and his wife coming back with the animals.

I. L. B.

LOWER CANYON, *September 21.*

We never reached Estes Park. There is no trail, and horses have never been across. We started from camp at ten, and spent four hours in searching for the trail. Chalmers tried gulch after gulch again, his self-assertion giving way a little after each failure; sometimes going east when

BAD FOOTING FOR HORSES

we should have gone west, always being brought up by a precipice or other impossibility. At last he went off by himself, and returned rejoicing, saying he had found the trail; and soon, sure enough, we were on a well-defined old trail, evidently made by carcasses which have been dragged along it by hunters. Vainly I pointed out to him that we were going north-east when we should have gone south-west, and that we were ascending instead of descending. "Oh, it's all right, and we shall soon come to water," he always replied. For two hours we ascended slowly through a thicket of aspen, the cold continually intensifying; but the trail, which had been growing fainter, died out, and an opening showed the top of Storm Peak not far off and not much above us, though it is 11,000 feet high. I could not help laughing. He had deliberately turned his back on Estes Park. He then confessed that he was lost, and that he could not find the way back. His wife sat down on the ground and cried bitterly. We ate some dry bread, and then I said I had had much experience in traveling, and would take the control of the party, which was agreed to, and we began the long descent. Soon after his wife was thrown from her horse, and cried bitterly again from fright and mortification. Soon after that the girth of the mule's saddle broke, and having no crupper, saddle and addenda went over his head, and the flour was dispersed. Next the girth of the woman's saddle broke, and she went over her horse's head. Then he began to fumble helplessly at it, railing against England the whole time, while I secured the saddle, and guided the route back to an outlet of the park. There a fire was built, and we had some bread and bacon; and then a search for water occupied nearly two hours, and resulted in the finding of a mud hole, trodden and defiled by hundreds of feet of elk, bears, cats, deer, and other beasts, and containing only a few gallons of water as thick as pea soup, with which we watered our animals and made some strong tea.

The sun was setting in glory as we started for the four hours' ride home, and the frost was intense, and made our bruised, grazed limbs ache painfully. I was sorry for Mrs. Chalmers, who had had several falls, and bore her aches patiently, and had said several times to her husband, with a kind meaning, "I am real sorry for this woman." I was so tired with the perpetual stumbling of my horse, as well as stiffened with the bitter cold, that I walked for the last hour or two; and Chalmers, as if to cover his failure, indulged in loud, incessant talk, abusing all other religionists, and railing against England in the coarsest American fashion. Yet, after all, they were not bad souls; and though he failed so grotesquely, he did his incompetent best. The log fire in the ruinous cabin was cheery, and I kept it up all night, and watched the stars through the holes in the roof, and thought of Long's Peak in its glorious solitude, and resolved that, come what might, I would reach Estes Park.

I. L. B.

Letter VI

Lower Canyon, *September 25.*

This is another world. My entrance upon it was signalized in this fashion. Chalmers offered me a *bronco* mare for a reasonable sum, and though she was a shifty, half-broken young thing, I came over here on her to try her, when, just as I was going away, she took into her head to "scare" and "buck," and when I touched her with my foot she leaped over a heap of timber, and the girth gave way, and the onlookers tell me that while she jumped I fell over her tail from a good height upon the hard gravel, receiving a parting kick on my knee. They could hardly believe that no bones were broken. The flesh of my left arm looks crushed into a jelly, but cold-water dressings will soon bring it right; and a cut on my back bled profusely; and the bleeding, with many bruises and the general shake, have made me feel weak, but circumstances do not admit of "making a fuss," and I really think that the rents in my riding dress will prove the most important part of the accident.

The surroundings here are pleasing. The log cabin, on the top of which a room with a steep, ornamental Swiss roof has been built, is in a valley close to a clear, rushing river, which emerges a little higher up from an inaccessible chasm of great sublimity. One side of the valley is formed by cliffs and terraces of porphyry as red as the reddest new brick, and at sunset blazing into vermilion. Through rifts in the nearer ranges there are glimpses of pine-clothed peaks, which, towards twilight, pass through every shade of purple and violet. The sky and the earth combine to form a Wonderland every evening—such rich, velvety coloring in crimson and violet; such an orange, green, and vermilion sky; such scarlet and emerald clouds; such an extraordinary dryness and purity of atmosphere, and then the glorious afterglow which seems to blend earth and heaven! For color, the Rocky Mountains beat all I have seen. The air has been cold, but the sun bright and hot during the last few days.

The story of my host is a story of misfortune. It indicates who should *not* come to Colorado.[1] He and his wife are under thirty-five. The son of a London physician in large practice, with a liberal education in the largest sense of the word, unusual culture and accomplishments, and the partner of a physician in good practice in the second city in England, he showed symptoms which threatened pulmonary disease. In an evil hour he heard of Colorado with its "unrivalled climate, boundless resources," etc., and, fascinated not only by these material advantages, but

[1] The story is ended now. A few months after my visit Mrs. H. died a few days after her confinement, and was buried on the bleak hill side, leaving her husband with five children under six years old, and Dr. H. is a prosperous man on one of the sunniest islands of the Pacific, with the devoted Swiss friend as his second wife.

by the notion of being able to found or reform society on advanced social theories of his own, he became an emigrant. Mrs. Hughes is one of the most charming, and lovable women I have ever seen, and their marriage is an ideal one. Both are fitted to shine in any society, but neither had the slightest knowledge of domestic and farming details. Dr. H. did not know how to saddle or harness a horse. Mrs. H. did not know whether you should put an egg into cold or hot water when you meant to boil it! They arrived at Longmount, bought up this claim, rather for the beauty of the scenery than for any substantial advantages, were cheated in land, goods, oxen, everything, and, to the discredit of the settlers, seemed to be regarded as fair game. Everything has failed with them, and though they "rise early, and late take rest, and eat the bread of carefulness," they hardly keep their heads above water. A young Swiss girl, devoted to them both, works as hard as they do. They have one horse, no wagon, some poultry, and a few cows, but no "hired man." It is the hardest and least ideal struggle that I have ever seen made by educated people. They had all their experience to learn, and they have bought it by losses and hardships. That they have learnt so much surprises me. Dr. H. and these two ladies built the upper room and the addition to the house without help. He has cropped the land himself, and has learned the difficult art of milking cows. Mrs. H. makes all the clothes required for a family of six, and her evenings, when the hard day's work is done and she is ready to drop from fatigue, are spent in mending and patching. The day is one long *grind*, without rest or enjoyment, or the pleasure of chance intercourse with cultivated people. The few visitors who have "happened in" are the thrifty wives of prosperous settlers, full of housewifely pride, whose one object seems to be to make Mrs. H. feel her inferiority to themselves. I wish she did take a more genuine interest in the "coming-on" of the last calf, the prospects of the squash crop, and the yield and price of butter; but though she has learned to make excellent butter and bread, it is all against the grain. The children are delightful. The little boys are refined, courteous, childish gentlemen, with love and tenderness to their parents in all their words and actions. Never a rough or harsh word is heard within the house. But the atmosphere of struggles and difficulties has already told on these infants. They consider their mother in all things, going without butter when they think the stock is low, bringing in wood and water too heavy for them to carry, anxiously speculating on the winter prospect and the crops, yet withal the most childlike and innocent of children.

One of the most painful things in the Western States and Territories is the extinction of childhood. I have never seen any children, only debased imitations of men and women, cankered by greed and selfishness, and asserting and gaining complete independence of their parents at ten years old. The atmosphere in which they are brought up is one of greed, godlessness, and frequently of profanity. Consequently these sweet things seem like flowers in a desert.

Except for love, which here as everywhere raises life into the ideal, this is a wretched existence. The poor crops have been destroyed by grasshoppers over and over again, and that talent deified here under the name of "smartness" has taken advantage of Dr. H. in all bargains, leaving him with little except food for his children. Experience has been dearly bought in all ways, and this instance of failure might be a useful warning to professional men without agricultural experience not to come and try to make a living by farming in Colorado.

My time here has passed very delightfully in spite of my regret and anxiety for this interesting family. I should like to stay longer, were it not that they have given up to me their straw bed, and Mrs. H. and her baby, a wizened, fretful child, sleep on the floor in my room, and Dr. H. on the floor downstairs, and the nights are frosty and chill. Work is the order of their day, and of mine, and at night, when the children are in bed, we three ladies patch the clothes and make shirts, and Dr. H. reads Tennyson's poems, or we speak tenderly of that world of culture and noble deeds which seems here "the land very far off," or Mrs. H. lays aside her work for a few minutes and reads some favorite passage of prose or poetry, as I have seldom heard either read before, with a voice of large compass and exquisite tone, quick to interpret every shade of the author's meaning, and soft, speaking eyes, moist with feeling and sympathy. These are our halcyon hours, when we forget the needs of the morrow, and that men still buy, sell, cheat, and strive for gold, and that we are in the Rocky Mountains, and that it is near midnight. But morning comes hot and tiresome, and the never-ending work is oppressive, and Dr. H. comes in from the field two or three times in the day, dizzy and faint, and they condole with each other, and I feel that the Colorado settler needs to be made of sterner stuff and to possess more adaptability.

To-day has been a very pleasant day for me, though I have only once sat down since 9 A.M., and it is now 5 P.M. I plotted that the devoted Swiss girl should go to the nearest settlement with two of the children for the day in a neighbor's wagon, and that Dr. and Mrs. H. should get an afternoon of rest and sleep upstairs, while I undertook to do the work and make something of a cleaning. I had a large "wash" of my own, having been hindered last week by my bad arm, but a clothes wringer which screws on to the side of the tub is a great assistance, and by folding the clothes before passing them through it, I make it serve instead of mangle and iron. After baking the bread and thoroughly cleaning the churn and pails, I began upon the tins and pans, the cleaning of which had fallen into arrears, and was hard at work, very greasy and grimy, when a man came in to know where to ford the river with his ox team, and as I was showing him he looked pityingly at me, saying, "Be you the new hired girl? Bless me, you're awful small!"

Yesterday we saved three cwt. of tomatoes for winter use, and about two tons of squash and pumpkin for the cattle, two of the former weighing 140 lbs. I pulled nearly a quarter of an acre of maize, but it was a scanty crop, and the husks were poorly filled. I much prefer field work to the scouring of greasy pans and to the wash tub, and both to either sewing or writing.

This is not Arcadia. "Smartness," which consists in over-reaching your neighbor in every fashion which is not illegal, is the quality which is held in the greatest repute, and Mammon is the divinity. From a generation brought up to worship the one and admire the other little can be hoped. In districts distant as this is from "Church Ordinances," there are three ways in which Sunday is spent: one, to make it a day for visiting, hunting, and fishing; another, to spend it in sleeping and abstinence from work;

and the third, to continue all the usual occupations, consequently harvesting and felling and hauling timber are to be seen in progress. Last Sunday a man came here and put up a door, and said he didn't believe in the Bible or in a God, and he wasn't going to sacrifice his children's bread to old-fashioned prejudices. There is a manifest indifference to the higher obligations of the law, "judgment, mercy and faith"; but in the main the settlers are steady, there are few flagrant breaches of morals, industry is the rule, life and property are far safer than in England or Scotland, and the law of universal respect to women is still in full force.

The days are now brilliant and the nights sharply frosty. People are preparing for the winter. The tourists from the East are trooping into Denver, and the surveying parties are coming down from the mountains. Snow has fallen on the higher ranges, and my hopes of getting to Estes Park are down at zero.

LONGMOUNT, *September 25.*

Yesterday was perfect. The sun was brilliant and the air cool and bracing. I felt better, and after a hard day's work and an evening stroll with my friends in the glorious afterglow, I went to bed cheerful and hopeful as to the climate and its effect on my health. This morning I awoke with a sensation of extreme lassitude, and on going out, instead of the delicious atmosphere of yesterday, I found intolerable suffocating heat, a *blazing* (not *brilliant*) sun, and a sirocco like a Victorian hot wind. Neuralgia, inflamed eyes, and a sense of extreme prostration followed, and my acclimatized hosts were somewhat similarly affected. The sparkle, the crystalline atmosphere, and the glory of color of yesterday, had all vanished. We had borrowed a wagon, but Dr. H.'s strong but lazy horse and a feeble hired one made a poor span; and though the distance here is only twenty-two miles over level prairie, our tired animal, and losing the way three times, have kept us eight and a half hours in the broiling sun. All notions of locality fail me on the prairie, and Dr. H. was not much better. We took wrong tracks, got entangled among fences, plunged through the deep mud of irrigation ditches, and were despondent. It was a miserable drive, sitting on a heap of fodder under the angry sun. Half-way here we camped at a river, now only a series of mud holes, and I fell asleep under the imperfect shade of a cotton-wood tree, dreading the thought of waking and jolting painfully along over the dusty prairie in the dust-laden, fierce sirocco, under the ferocious sun. We never saw man or beast the whole day.

This is the "Chicago Colony," and it is said to be prospering, after some preliminary land swindles. It is as uninviting as Fort Collins. We first came upon dust-colored frame houses set down at intervals on the dusty buff plain, each with its dusty wheat or barley field adjacent, the crop, not the product of the rains of heaven, but of the muddy overflow of "Irrigating Ditch No. 2." Then comes a road made up of many converging wagon tracks, which stiffen into a wide straggling street, in which glaring frame houses and a few shops stand opposite to each other. A two-storey house, one of the whitest and most glaring, and without a veranda like all the others, is the "St. Vrain Hotel," called after the St. Vrain River, out of which the ditch is taken which enables Longmount to exist. Everything was broiling in the heat of the slanting sun, which all day long had been beating on the unshaded wooden rooms. The heat within was more sickening than outside, and black flies covered everything, one's face included. We all sat fighting the flies in my bedroom, which was cooler than elsewhere, till a glorious sunset over the Rocky Range, some ten miles off, compelled us to go out and enjoy it. Then followed supper, Western fashion, without table-cloths, and all the "unattached" men of Longmount came in and fed silently and rapidly. It was a great treat to have tea to drink, as I had not tasted any for a fortnight. The landlord is a jovial, kindly man. I told him how my plans had failed, and how I was reluctantly going on to-morrow to Denver and New York, being unable to get to Estes Park, and he said there might yet be a chance of some one coming in to-night who would be going up. He soon came to my room and asked definitely what I could do—if I feared cold, if I could "rough it," if I could "ride horse-back and lope." Estes Park and its surroundings are, he says, "the most beautiful scenery in Colorado," and "it's a real shame," he added, "for you not to see it." We had hardly sat down to tea when he came, saying "You're in luck this time; two young men have just come in and are going up to-morrow morning." I am rather pleased, and have hired a horse for three days; but I am not very hope-ful, for I am almost ill of the smothering heat, and still suffer from my fall, and not having been on horseback since, thirty miles will be a long ride. Then I fear that the accommodation is as rough as Chalmer's, and that solitude will be impossible. We have been strolling in the street every since it grew dark to get the little air which is moving.

ESTES PARK!!! *September 28.*

I wish I could let those three notes of admiration go to
you instead of a letter. They mean everything that is
rapturous and delightful—grandeur, cheerfulness, health,
enjoyment, novelty, freedom, etc., etc. I have just dropped
into the very place I have been seeking, but in everything
it exceeds all my dreams. There is health in every breath
of air; I am much better already, and get up to a seven
o'clock breakfast without difficulty. It is quite comfortable—in the fashion that I like. I have a log cabin, raised on
six posts, all to myself, with a skunk's lair underneath it,
and a small lake close to it. There is a frost every night,
and all day it is cool enough for a roaring fire. The ranch-
man, who is half-hunter, half-stockman, and his wife are
jovial, hearty Welsh people from Llanberis, who laugh
with loud, cheery British laughs, sing in parts down to the
youngest child, are free hearted and hospitable, and pile
the pitch-pine logs half-way up the great rude chimney.
There has been fresh meat each day since I came, delicious
bread baked daily, excellent potatoes, tea and coffee, and
an abundant supply of milk like cream. I have a clean hay
bed with six blankets, and there are neither bugs nor fleas.
The scenery is the most glorious I have ever seen, and is
above us, around us, at the very door. Most people have
advized me to go to Colorado Springs, and only one mentioned this place, and till I reached Longmount I never
saw any one who had been here, but I saw from the lie of
the country that it must be most superbly situated. People
said, however, that it was most difficult of access, and that
the season for it was over. In traveling there is nothing
like dissecting people's statements, which are usually col-

73

ored by their estimate of the powers or likings of the person spoken to, making all reasonable inquiries, and then pertinaciously but quietly carrying out one's own plans. This is perfection, and all the requisites for health are present, including plenty of horses and grass to ride on.

It is not easy to sit down to write after ten hours of hard riding, especially in a cabin full of people, and wholesome fatigue may make my letter flat when it ought to be enthusiastic. I was awake all night at Longmount owing to the stifling heat, and got up nervous and miserable, ready to give up the thought of coming here, but the sunrise over the Plains, and the wonderful red of the Rocky Mountains, as they reflected the eastern sky, put spirit into me. The landlord had got a horse, but could not give any satisfactory assurances of his being quiet, and being much shaken by my fall at Canyon, I earnestly wished that the *Greeley Tribune* had not given me a reputation for horsemanship, which had preceded me here. The young men who were to escort me "seemed very innocent," he said, but I have not arrived at his meaning yet. When the horse appeared in the street at 8:30, I saw, to my dismay, a high-bred, beautiful creature, stable kept, with arched neck, quivering nostrils, and restless ears and eyes. My pack, as on Hawaii, was strapped behind the Mexican saddle, and my canvas bag hung on the horn, but the horse did not look fit to carry "gear," and seemed to require two men to hold and coax him. There were many loafers about, and I shrank from going out and mounting in my old Hawaiian riding dress, though Dr. and Mrs. H. assured me that I looked quite "insignificant and unnoticeable." We got away at nine with repeated injunctions from the landlord in the words, "Oh, you should be heroic!"

74

The sky was cloudless, and a deep brilliant blue, and though the sun was hot the air was fresh and bracing. The ride for glory and delight I shall label along with one to Hanalei, and another to Mauna Kea, Hawaii. I felt better quite soon; the horse in gait and temper turned out perfection—all spring and spirit, elastic in his motion, walking fast and easily, and cantering with a light, graceful swing as soon as one pressed the reins on his neck, a blithe, joyous animal, to whom a day among the mountains seemed a pleasant frolic. So gentle he was, that when I got off and walked he followed me without being led, and without needing any one to hold him he allowed me to mount on either side. In addition to the charm of his movements he has the catlike sure-footedness of a Hawaiian horse, and fords rapid and rough-bottomed rivers, and gallops among stones and stumps, and down steep hills, with equal security. I could have ridden him a hundred miles as easily as thirty. We have only been together two days, yet we are firm friends, and thoroughly understand each other. I should not require another companion on a long mountain tour. All his ways are those of an animal brought up without curb, whip, or spur, trained by the voice, and used only to kindness, as is happily the case with the majority of horses in the Western States. Consequently, unless they are *broncos*, they exercise their intelligence for your advantage, and do their work rather as friends than as machines.

I soon began not only to feel better, but to be exhilarated with the delightful motion. The sun was behind us, and puffs of a cool elastic air came down from the glorious mountains in front. We cantered across six miles of prairie, and then reached the beautiful canyon of the St. Vrain, which, towards its mouth, is a narrow, fertile, wooded valley, through which a bright rapid river, which we forded many times, hurries along, with twists and windings innumerable. Ah, how brightly its ripples danced in the glittering sunshine, and how musically its waters murmured like the streams of windward Hawaii! We lost our way over and over again, though the "innocent" young men had been there before; indeed, it would require some talent to master the intricacies of that devious trail, but settlers making hay always appeared in the nick of time to put us on the right track. Very fair it was, after the brown and burning plains, and the variety was endless. Cotton-wood trees were green and bright, aspens shivered in gold tremulousness, wild grape-vines trailed their lemon-colored foliage along the ground, and the Virginia creeper hung its crimson sprays here and there, lightening up green and gold into glory. Sometimes from under the cool and bowery shade of the colored tangle we passed into the cool St. Vrain, and then were wedged between its margin and lofty cliffs and terraces of incredibly staring, fantastic rocks, lined, patched, and splashed with carmine, vermilion, greens of all tints, blue, yellow, orange, violet, deep crimson, coloring that no artist would dare to represent, and of which, in sober prose, I scarcely dare tell. Long's wonderful peaks, which hitherto had gleamed above the green, now disappeared, to be seen no more for twenty miles. We entered on an ascending valley, where the gorgeous hues of the rocks were intensified by the blue gloom of the pitch pines, and then taking a track to the north-west, we left the softer world behind, and all traces of man and his works, and plunged into the Rocky Mountains.

There were wonderful ascents then up which I led my horse; wild fantastic views opening up continually, a recurrence of surprises; the air keener and purer with every mile, the sensation of loneliness more singular. A tremendous ascent among rocks and pines to a height of 9,000 feet brought us to a passage seven feet wide through a wall of rock, with an abrupt descent of 2,000 feet, and a yet higher ascent beyond. I never saw anything so strange as looking back. It was a single gigantic ridge which we had passed through, standing up knifelike, built up entirely of great brick-shaped masses of bright red rock, some of them as large as the Royal Institution, Edinburgh, piled one on another by Titans. Pitch pines grew out of their crevices, but there was not a vestige of soil. Beyond, wall beyond wall of similar construction, and range above range, rose into the blue sky. Fifteen miles more over great ridges, along passes dark with shadow, and so narrow that we had to ride in the beds of the streams which had excavated them, round the bases of colossal pyramids of rock crested with pines, up into fair upland "parks," scarlet in patches with the poison oak, parks so beautifully arranged by nature that I momentarily expected to come upon some stately mansion, but that afternoon crested blue jays and chipmonks had them all to themselves. Here, in the early morning, deer, bighorn, and the stately elk, come down to feed, and there, in the night, prowl and growl the Rocky Mountain lion, the grizzly bear, and the cowardly wolf. There were chasms of immense depth, dark with the indigo gloom of pines, and mountains with snow gleaming on their splintered crests, loveliness to bewilder and grandeur to awe, and still streams and shady pools, and cool depths of shadow; mountains again, dense

77

with pines, among which patches of aspen gleamed like gold; valleys where the yellow cotton-wood mingled with the crimson oak, and so, on and on through the lengthening shadows, till the trail, which in places had been hardly legible, became well defined, and we entered a long gulch with broad swellings of grass belted with pines.

A very pretty mare, hobbled, was feeding; a collie dog barked at us, and among the scrub, not far from the track, there was a rude, black log cabin, as rough as it could be to be a shelter at all, with smoke coming out of the roof and window. We diverged towards it; it mattered not that it was the home, or rather den, of a notorious "ruffian" and "desperado." One of my companions had disappeared hours before, the remaining one was a town-bred youth. I longed to speak to some one who loved the mountains. I called the hut a *den*—it looked like the den of a wild beast. The big dog lay outside it in a threatening attitude and growled. The mud roof was covered with lynx, beaver, and other furs laid out to dry, beaver paws were pinned out on the logs, a part of the carcass of a deer hung at one end of the cabin, a skinned beaver lay in front of a heap of peltry just within the door, and antlers of deer, old horseshoes, and offal of many animals, lay about the den.

Roused by the growling of the dog, his owner came out, a broad, thickset man, about the middle height, with an old cap on his head, and wearing a grey hunting suit much the worse for wear (almost falling to pieces, in fact), a digger's scarf knotted round his waist, a knife in his belt, and "a bosom friend," a revolver, sticking out of the breast pocket of his coat; his feet, which were very small, were bare, except for some dilapidated moccasins made of horse hide. The marvel was how his clothes hung

78

together, and on him. The scarf round his waist must have had something to do with it. His face was remarkable. He is a man about forty-five, and must have been strikingly handsome. He has large grey-blue eyes, deeply set, with well-marked eyebrows, a handsome aquiline nose, and a very handsome mouth. His face was smooth shaven except for a dense mustache and imperial. Tawny hair, in thin uncared-for curls, fell from under his hunter's cap and over his collar. One eye was entirely gone, and the loss made one side of the face repulsive, while the other might have been modeled in marble. "Desperado" was written in large letters all over him. I almost repented of having sought his acquaintance. His first impulse was to swear at the dog, but on seeing a lady he contented himself with kicking him, and coming to me he raised his cap, showing as he did so a magnificently-formed brow and head, and in a cultured tone of voice asked if there were anything he could do for me? I asked for some water, and he brought some in a battered tin, gracefully apologizing for not having anything more presentable. We entered into conversation, and as he spoke I forgot both his reputation and appearance, for his manner was that of a chivalrous gentleman, his accent refined, and his language easy and elegant. I inquired about some beavers' paws which were drying, and in a moment they hung on the horn of my saddle. *Apropos* of the wild animals of the region, he told me that the loss of his eye was owing to a recent encounter with a grizzly bear, which, after giving him a death hug, tearing him all over, breaking his arm and scratching out his eye, had left him for dead. As we rode away, for the sun was sinking, he said, courteously, "You are not an American. I know from your voice that you are a country-

79

woman of mine. I hope you will allow me the pleasure of calling on you."[2]

This man, known through the Territories and beyond them as "Rocky Mountain Jim," or, more briefly, as "Mountain Jim," is one of the famous scouts of the Plains, and is the original of some daring portraits in fiction concerning Indian Frontier warfare. So far as I have at present heard, he is a man for whom there is now no room, for the time for blows and blood in this part of Colorado is past, and the fame of many daring exploits is sullied by crimes which are not easily forgiven here. He now has a "squatter's claim," but makes his living as a trapper, and is a complete child of the mountains. Of his genius and chivalry to women there does not appear to be any doubt; but he is a desperate character, and is subject to "ugly fits," when people think it best to avoid him. It is here regarded as an evil that he has located himself at the mouth of the only entrance to the park, for he is dangerous with his pistols, and it would be safer if he were not here. His besetting sin is indicated in the verdict pronounced on him by my host: "When he's sober Jim's a perfect gentleman; but when he's had liquor he's the most awful ruffian in Colorado."

From the ridge on which this gulch terminates, at a

[2] Of this unhappy man, who was shot nine months later within two miles of his cabin, I write in the subsequent letters only as he appeared to me. His life, without doubt, was deeply stained with crimes and vices, and his reputation for ruffianism was a deserved one. But in my intercourse with him I saw more of his nobler instincts than of the darker parts of his character, which, unfortunately for himself and others, showed itself in its worst colors at the time of his tragic end. It was not until after I left Colorado, not indeed until after his death, that I heard of the worst points of his character.

height of 9,000 feet, we saw at last Estes Park, lying 1,500 feet below in the glory of the setting sun, an irregular basin, lighted up by the bright waters of the rushing Thompson, guarded by sentinel mountains of fantastic shape and monstrous size, with Long's Peak rising above them all in unapproachable grandeur, while the Snowy Range, with its outlying spurs heavily timbered, come down upon the park slashed by stupendous canyons lying deep in purple gloom. The rushing river was blood red, Long's Peak was aflame, the glory of the glowing heaven was given back from earth. Never, nowhere, have I seen anything to equal the view into Estes Park. The mountains "of the land which is very far off" are very near now, but the near is more glorious than the far, and reality than dreamland. The mountain fever seized me, and, giving my tireless horse one encouraging word, he dashed at full gallop over a mile of smooth sward at delirious speed.

But I was hungry, and the air was frosty, and I was wondering what the prospects of food and shelter were in this enchanted region, when we came suddenly upon a small lake, close to which was a very trim-looking log cabin, with a flat mud roof, with four smaller ones; picturesquely dotted about near it, two corrals,[3] a long shed, in front of which a steer was being killed, a log dairy with a water wheel, some hay piles, and various evidences of comfort; and two men, on serviceable horses, were just bringing in some tolerable cows to be milked. A short, pleasant-looking man ran up to me and shook hands glee-

[3] A *corral* is a fenced enclosure for cattle. This word, with *bronco*, *ranch*, and a few others, are adaptations from the Spanish, and are used as extensively throughout California and the Territories as is the Spanish or Mexican saddle.

fully, which surprised me; but he has since told me that in the evening light he thought I was "Mountain Jim, dressed up as a woman!" I recognized in him a country-man, and he introduced himself as Griffith Evans, a Welsh-man from the slate quarries near Llanberis. When the cabin door was opened I saw a good-sized log room, un-chinked, however, with windows of infamous glass, look-ing two ways; a rough stone fireplace, in which pine logs, half as large as I am, were burning; a boarded floor, a round table, two rocking chairs, a carpet-covered back-woods couch; and skins, Indian bows and arrows, wam-pum belts, and antlers, fitly decorated the rough walls, and equally fitly, rifles were stuck up in the corners. Seven men, smoking, were lying about on the floor, a sick man lay on the couch, and a middle-aged lady sat at the table writing. I went out again and asked Evans if he could take me in, expecting nothing better than a shakedown; but, to my joy, he told me he could give me a cabin to myself, two minutes' walk from his own. So in this glorious upper world, with the mountain pines behind and the clear lake in front, in the "blue hollow at the foot of Long's Peak," at a height of 7,500 feet, where the hoar frost crisps the grass every night of the year, I have found far more than I ever dared to hope for.

I. L. B.

Letter VII

ESTES PARK, COLORADO, *October*.

As this account of the ascent of Long's Peak could not be written at the time, I am much disinclined to write it, especially as no sort of description within my powers could enable another to realize the glorious sublimity, the majestic solitude, and the unspeakable awfulness and fascination of the scenes in which I spent Monday, Tuesday, and Wednesday.

Long's Peak, 14,700 feet high, blocks up one end of Estes Park, and dwarfs all the surrounding mountains. From it on this side rise, snow-born, the bright St. Vrain, and the Big and Little Thompson. By sunlight or moonlight its splintered grey crest is the one object which, in spite of wapiti and bighorn, skunk and grizzly, unfailingly arrests the eyes. From it come all storms of snow and wind, and the forked lightnings play round its head like a glory. It is one of the noblest of mountains, but in one's imagination it grows to be much more than a mountain. It becomes invested with a personality. In its caverns and abysses one comes to fancy that it generates and chains the strong winds, to let them loose in its fury. The thunder becomes its voice, and the lightnings do it homage. Other summits blush under the morning kiss of the sun, and turn pale the next moment; but it detains the first sunlight and holds it round its head for an hour at least, till it pleases to change from rosy red to deep blue; and the sunset, as if spell-bound, lingers latest on its crest. The soft winds which hardly rustle the pine needles down here are raging rudely up there round its motionless summit. The mark of fire is upon it; and though it has passed into a grim repose, it tells of fire and upheaval as truly, though not as eloquently, as the living volcanoes of Hawaii. Here under its shadow one learns how naturally nature worship, and the propitiation of the forces of nature, arose in minds which had no better light.

Long's Peak, "the American Matterhorn," as some call it, was ascended five years ago for the first time. I thought I should like to attempt it, but up to Monday, when Evans left for Denver, cold water was thrown upon the project. It was too late in the season, the winds were likely to be strong, etc.; but just before leaving, Evans said that the weather was looking more settled, and if I did not get farther than the timber line it would be worth going. Soon after he left, "Mountain Jim" came in, and he would go up as guide, and the two youths who rode here with me from Longmount and I caught at the proposal. Mrs. Edwards at once baked bread for three days, steaks were cut from the steer which hangs up conveniently, and tea, sugar, and butter were benevolently added. Our picnic was not to be a luxurious or "well-found" one, for, in order to avoid the expense of a pack mule, we limited our luggage to what our saddle horses could carry. Behind my saddle I carried three pair of camping blankets and a quilt, which reached to my shoulders. My own boots were so much worn that it was painful to walk, even about the park, in them, so Evans had lent me a pair of his hunting boots, which hung to the horn of my saddle. The horses of the two young men were equally loaded, for we had to prepare for many degrees of frost. "Jim" was a shocking figure; he had on an old pair of high boots, with a baggy pair of old trousers made of deer hide, held on by an old scarf tucked into them; a leather shirt, with three or four ragged unbuttoned waistcoats over it; an old smashed wideawake, from under which his tawny, neglected ringlets hung; and with his one eye, his one long spur, his knife in his belt, his revolver in his waistcoat pocket, his saddle covered with an old beaver skin, from which the paws hung down; his camping blankets behind him, his rifle laid across the saddle in front of him, and his axe, canteen, and other gear hanging to the horn, he was as awful-looking a ruffian as one could see. By way of contrast he rode a small Arab mare, of exquisite beauty, skittish, high spirited, gentle, but altogether too light for him, and he fretted her incessantly to make her display herself.

Heavily loaded as all our horses were, "Jim" started over the half-mile of level grass at a hard gallop, and then throwing his mare on her haunches, pulled up alongside of me, and with a grace of manner which soon made me forget his appearance, entered into a conversation which lasted for more than three hours, in spite of the manifold checks of fording streams, single file, abrupt ascents and descents, and other incidents of mountain travel. The ride was one series of glories and surprises, of "park" and glade, of lake and stream, of mountains on mountains, culminating in the rent pinnacles of Long's Peak, which looked yet grander and ghastlier as we crossed an attendant mountain 11,000 feet high. The slanting sun added fresh beauty every hour. There were dark pines against a lemon sky, grey peaks reddening and etherealizing, gorges of deep and infinite blue, floods of golden glory pouring through canyons of enormous depth, an atmosphere of absolute purity, an occasional foreground of cotton-wood and aspen flaunting in red and gold to intensify the blue gloom of the pines, the trickle and murmur of streams fringed with icicles, the strange *sough* of gusts moving among the pine tops—sights and sounds not of the lower earth, but of the solitary, beast-haunted, frozen upper altitudes. From the dry, buff grass of Estes Park we turned off up a trail on the side of a pine-hung gorge, up a steep pine-clothed hill, down to a small valley, rich in fine, sun-cured hay about eighteen inches high, and enclosed by high mountains whose deepest hollow contains a lily-covered lake, fitly named "The Lake of the Lilies." Ah, how magical its beauty was, as it slept in silence, while *there* the dark pines were mirrored motionless in its pale gold, and *here* the great white lily cups and dark green leaves rested on amethyst-colored water!

From this we ascended into the purple gloom of great pine forests which clothe the skirts of the mountains up to a height of about 11,000 feet, and from their chill and solitary depths we had glimpses of golden atmosphere and rose-lit summits, not of "the land very far off," but of the land nearer now in all its grandeur, gaining in sublimity by nearness—glimpses, too, through a broken vista of purple gorges, of the illimitable Plains lying idealized in the late sunlight, their baked, brown expanse transfigured into the likeness of a sunset sea rolling infinitely in waves of misty gold.

We rode upwards through the gloom on a steep trail blazed through the forest, all my intellect concentrated on avoiding being dragged off my horse by impending branches, or having the blankets badly torn, as those of my companions were, by sharp dead limbs, between which there was hardly room to pass—the horses breathless, and requiring to stop every few yards, though their riders, except myself, were afoot. The gloom of the dense, ancient, silent forest is to me awe inspiring. On such an evening it is soundless, except for the branches creaking in the soft wind, the frequent snap of decayed timber, and a murmur in the pine tops as of a not distant waterfall, all tending to produce *eeriness* and a sadness "hardly akin to pain." There no lumberer's axe has ever rung. The trees die when they have attained their prime, and stand there, dead and bare, till the fierce mountain winds lay them prostrate. The pines grew smaller and more sparse as we ascended, and the last stragglers wore a tortured, warring look. The timber line was passed, but yet a little higher a slope of mountain meadow dipped to the south-west towards a bright stream trickling under ice and icicles, and there a grove of the beautiful silver spruce marked our camping ground. The trees were in miniature, but so exquisitely arranged that one might well ask what artist's hand had planted them, scattering them here, clumping them there, and training their slim spires towards heaven. Hereafter, when I call up memories of the glorious, the view from this camping ground will come up. Looking east, gorges opened to the distant Plains, then fading into

GRAND CRATER

purple grey. Mountains with pine-clothed skirts rose in ranges, or, solitary, uplifted their grey summits, while close behind, but nearly 3,000 feet above us, towered the bald white crest of Long's Peak, its huge precipices red with the light of a sun long lost to our eyes. Close to us, in the caverned side of the Peak, was snow that, owing to its position, is eternal. Soon the afterglow came on, and before it faded a big half-moon hung out of the heavens, shining through the silver blue foliage of the pines on the frigid background of snow, and turning the whole into fairyland. The "photo" which accompanies this letter is by a courageous Denver artist who attempted the ascent just before I arrived, but, after camping out at the timber line for a week, was foiled by the perpetual storms, and was driven down again, leaving some very valuable apparatus about 3,000 feet from the summit.

Unsaddling and picketing the horses securely, making the beds of pine shoots, and dragging up logs for fuel, warmed us all. "Jim" built up a great fire, and before long we were all sitting around it at supper. It didn't matter much that we had to drink our tea out of the battered meat tins in which it was boiled, and eat strips of beef reeking with pine smoke without plates or forks.

"Treat Jim as a gentleman and you'll find him one," I had been told; and though his manner was certainly bolder and freer than that of gentlemen generally, no imaginary fault could be found. He was very agreeable as a man of culture as well as a child of nature; the desperado was altogether out of sight. He was very courteous and even kind to me, which was fortunate, as the young men had little idea of showing even ordinary civilities. That night I made the acquaintance of his dog "Ring," said to be the best hunting dog in Colorado, with the body and legs of a collie, but a head approaching that of a mastiff, a noble face with a wistful human expression, and the most truthful eyes I ever saw in an animal. His master loves him if he loves anything, but in his savage moods ill-treats him. "Ring's" devotion never swerves, and his truthful eyes are rarely taken off his master's face. He is almost human in his intelligence, and, unless he is told to do so, he never takes notice of any one but "Jim." In a tone as if speaking to a human being, his master, pointing to me, said, "Ring, go to that lady, and don't leave her again to-night." "Ring" at once came to me, looked into my face, laid his head on my shoulder, and then lay down beside me with his head on my lap, but never taking his eyes from "Jim's" face.

The long shadows of the pines lay upon the frosted grass, an aurora leaped fitfully, and the moonlight, though intensely bright, was pale beside the red, leaping flames of our pine logs and their red glow on our gear, ourselves, and Ring's truthful face. One of the young men sang a Latin student's song and two Negro melodies; the other "Sweet Spirit, hear my Prayer." "Jim" sang one of Moore's melodies in a singular falsetto, and all together sang, "The Star-spangled Banner" and "The Red, White, and Blue." Then "Jim" recited a very clever poem of his own composition, and told some fearful Indian stories. A group of small silver spruces away from the fire was my sleeping place. The artist who had been up there had so woven and interlaced their lower branches as to form a bower, affording at once shelter from the wind and a most agreeable privacy. It was thickly strewn with young pine shoots, and these, when covered with a blanket, with an inverted saddle for a pillow, made a luxurious bed. The mercury at 9 P.M. was 12° below the freezing point. "Jim," after a last look at the horses, made a huge fire, and stretched himself out beside it, but "Ring" lay at my back to keep me warm. I could not sleep, but the night passed rapidly. I was anxious about the ascent, for gusts of ominous sound swept through the pines at intervals. Then wild animals howled, and "Ring" was perturbed in spirit about them. Then it was strange to see the notorious desperado, a red-handed man, sleeping as quietly as innocence sleeps. But, above all, it was exciting to lie there, with no better shelter than a bower of pines, on a mountain 11,000 feet high, in the very heart of the Rocky Range, under twelve degrees of frost, hearing sounds of wolves, with shivering stars looking through the fragrant canopy, with arrowy pines for bed-posts, and for a night lamp the red flames of a camp-fire.

Day dawned long before the sun rose, pure and lemon colored. The rest were looking after the horses, when one of the students came running to tell me that I must come farther down the slope, for "Jim" said he had never seen such a sunrise. From the chill, grey Peak above, from the everlasting snows, from the silvered pines, down through mountain ranges with their depths of Tyrian purple, we looked to where the Plains lay cold, in blue-grey, like a morning sea against a far horizon. Suddenly, as a dazzling streak at first, but enlarging rapidly into a dazzling sphere, the sun wheeled above the grey line, a light and glory as when it was first created. "Jim" involuntarily and reverently uncovered his head, and exclaimed, "I believe there is a God!" I felt as if, Parsee-like, I must worship. The grey of the Plains changed to purple, the sky was all one rose-red flush, on which vermilion cloud-streaks rested; the

LAVA BEDS, LONG'S PEAK

ghastly peaks gleamed like rubies, the earth and heavens were new created. Surely "the Most High dwelleth not in temples made with hands!" For a full hour those Plains simulated the ocean, down to whose limitless expanse of purple, cliff, rocks, and promontories swept down.

By seven we had finished breakfast, and passed into the ghastlier solitudes above, I riding as far as what, rightly or wrongly, are called the "Lava Beds," an expanse of large and small boulders, with snow in their crevices. It was very cold; some water which we crossed was frozen hard enough to bear the horse. "Jim" had advised me against taking any wraps, and my thin Hawaiian riding dress, only fit for the tropics, was penetrated by the keen air. The rarefied atmosphere soon began to oppress our breathing, and I found that Evans's boots were so large that I had no foothold. Fortunately, before the real difficulty of the ascent began, we found, under a rock, a pair of small overshoes, probably left by the Hayden exploring expedition, which just lasted for the day. As we were leaping from rock to rock, "Jim" said, "I was thinking in the night about your traveling alone, and wondering where you carried your Derringer, for I could see no signs of it." On my telling him that I traveled unarmed, he could hardly believe it, and adjured me to get a revolver at once.

On arriving at the "Notch" (a literal gate of rock), we found ourselves absolutely on the knifelike ridge or backbone of Long's Peak, only a few feet wide, covered with colossal boulders and fragments, and on the other side shelving in one precipitous, snow-patched sweep of 3,000 feet to a picturesque hollow, containing a lake of pure green water. Other lakes, hidden among dense pine woods, were farther off, while close above us rose the Peak, which, for about 500 feet, is a smooth, gaunt, inaccessible-looking pile of granite. Passing through the "Notch," we looked along the nearly inaccessible side of the Peak, composed of boulders and *débris* of all shapes and sizes, through which appeared broad, smooth ribs of reddish-colored granite, looking as if they upheld the towering rock mass above. I usually dislike bird's-eye and panoramic views, but, though from a mountain, this was not one. Serrated ridges, not much lower than that on which we stood, rose, one beyond another, far as that pure atmosphere could carry the vision, broken into awful chasms deep with ice and snow, rising into pinnacles piercing the heavenly blue with their cold, barren grey, on, on for ever, till the most distant range upbore unsullied snow alone. There were fair lakes mirroring the dark pine woods, canyons dark and blue-black with unbroken expanses of pines, snow-slashed pinnacles, wintry heights frowning upon lovely parks, watered and wooded, lying in the lap of summer; North Park floating off into the blue distance, Middle Park closed till another season, the sunny slopes of Estes Park, and winding down among the mountains the snowy ridge of the Divide, whose bright waters seek both the Atlantic and Pacific Oceans. There, far below, links of diamonds showed where the Grand River takes its rise to seek the mysterious Colorado, with its still unsolved enigma, and lose itself in the waters of the Pacific; and nearer the snow-born Thompson bursts forth from the ice to begin its journey to the Gulf of Mexico. Nature, rioting in her grandest mood, exclaimed with voices of grandeur, solitude, sublimity, beauty, and infinity, "Lord, what is man, that Thou art mindful of him? or the son of man, that Thou visitest him?" Never-to-be-forgotten glories they were, burnt in upon my memory by six succeeding hours of terror.

You know I have no head and no ankles, and never ought to dream of mountaineering; and had I known that the ascent was a real mountaineering feat I should not have felt the slightest ambition to perform it. As it is, I am only humiliated by my success, for "Jim" dragged me up, like a bale of goods, by sheer force of muscle. At the "Notch" the real business of the ascent began. Two thousand feet of solid rock towered above us, four thousand feet of broken rock shelved precipitously below; smooth granite ribs, with barely foothold, stood out here and there; melted snow refrozen several times, presented a more serious obstacle; many of the rocks were loose, and tumbled down when touched. To me it was a time of extreme terror. I was roped to "Jim," but it was of no use; my feet were paralyzed and slipped on the bare rock, and he said it was useless to try to go that way, and we retraced our steps. I wanted to return to the "Notch," knowing that my incompetence would detain the party, and one of the young men said almost plainly that a woman was a dangerous encumbrance, but the trapper replied shortly that if it were not to take a lady up he would not go up at all. He went on the explore, and reported that further progress on the correct line of ascent was blocked by ice; and then for two hours we descended, lowering ourselves by our hands from rock to rock along a boulder-strewn sweep of 4,000 feet, patched with ice and snow, and perilous from rolling stones. My fatigue, giddiness, and pain from bruised ankles, and arms half pulled out of their sockets, were so great that I should never have gone halfway had not "Jim," *nolens volens*, dragged me along with a patience and skill, and withal a determination that I should ascend the Peak, which never failed. After descending about 2,000 feet to avoid the ice, we got into a deep ravine with inaccessible sides, partly filled with ice and snow and partly with large and small fragments of rock, which were constantly giving away, rendering the footing very insecure. That part to me was two hours of painful and unwilling submission to the inevitable; of trembling, slipping, straining, of smooth ice appearing when it was least expected, and of weak entreaties to be left behind while the others went on. "Jim" always said that there was no danger, that there was only a short bad bit ahead, and that I should go up even if he carried me!

Slipping, faltering, gasping from the exhausting toil in the rarefied air, with throbbing hearts and panting lungs, we reached the top of the gorge and squeezed ourselves between two gigantic fragments of rock by a passage called the "Dog's Lift," when I climbed on the shoulders of one man and then was hauled up. This introduced us by an abrupt turn round the south-west angle of the Peak to a narrow shelf of considerable length, rugged, uneven, and so overhung by the cliff in some places that it is necessary to crouch to pass at all. Above, the Peak looks nearly vertical for 400 feet; and below, the most tremendous precipice I have ever seen descends in one unbroken fall. This is usually considered the most dangerous part of the ascent, but it does not seem so to me, for such foothold as there is is secure, and one fancies that it is possible to hold on with the hands. But there, and on the final, and, to my thinking, the worst part of the climb, one slip, and a breathing, thinking, human being would lie 3,000 feet below, a shapeless, bloody heap! "Ring" refused to traverse the Ledge, and remained at the "Lift" howling piteously.

From thence the view is more magnificent even than that from the "Notch." At the foot of the precipice below us lay a lovely lake, wood embosomed, from or near which the bright St. Vrain and other streams take their rise. I thought how their clear cold waters, growing turbid in the affluent flats, would heat under the tropic sun, and eventually form part of that great ocean river which renders our far-off islands habitable by impinging on their shores. Snowy ranges, one behind the other, extended to the distant horizon, folding in their wintry embrace the beauties of Middle Park. Pike's Peak, more than one hundred miles off, lifted that vast but shapeless summit which is the landmark of southern Colorado. There were snow patches, snow slashes, snow abysses, snow forlorn and soiled looking, snow pure and dazzling, snow glistening above the purple robe of pine worn by all the mountains; while away to the east, in limitless breadth, stretched the green-grey of the endless Plains. Giants everywhere reared their splintered crests. From thence, with a single sweep, the eye takes in a distance of 300 miles—that distance to the west, north, and south being made up of mountains ten, eleven, twelve, and thirteen thousand feet in height, dominated by Long's Peak, Gray's Peak, and Pike's Peak, all nearly the height of Mont Blanc! On the Plains we traced the rivers by their fringe of cottonwoods to the distant Platte, and between us and them lay glories of mountain, canyon, and lake, sleeping in depths of blue and purple most ravishing to the eye.

As we crept from the ledge round a horn of rock I beheld what made me perfectly sick and dizzy to look at—the terminal Peak itself—a smooth, cracked face or wall of pink granite, as nearly perpendicular as anything could well be up which it was possible to climb, well deserving the name of the "American Matterhorn."[1]

Scaling, not climbing, is the correct term for this last ascent. It took one hour to accomplish 500 feet, pausing for breath every minute or two. The only foothold was in

[1] Let no practical mountaineer be allured by my description into the ascent of Long's Peak. Truly terrible as it was to me, to a member of the Alpine Club it would not be a feat worth performing.

narrow cracks or on minute projections on the granite. To get a toe in these cracks, or here and there on a scarcely obvious projection, while crawling on hands and knees, all the while tortured with thirst and gasping and struggling for breath, this was the climb; but at last the Peak was won. A grand, well-defined mountain top it is, a nearly level acre of boulders, with precipitous sides all round, the one we came up being the only accessible one.

It was not possible to remain long. One of the young men was seriously alarmed by bleeding from the lungs, and the intense dryness of the day and the rarefication of the air, at a height of nearly 15,000 feet, made respiration very painful. There is always water on the Peak, but it was frozen as hard as a rock, and the sucking of ice and snow increases thirst. We all suffered severely from the want of water, and the gasping for breath made our mouths and tongues so dry that articulation was difficult, and the speech of all unnatural.

From the summit were seen in unrivalled combination all the views which had rejoiced our eyes during the ascent. It was something at last to stand upon the storm-rent crown of this lonely sentinel of the Rocky Range, on one of the mightiest of the vertebrae of the backbone of the North American continent, and to see the waters start for both oceans. Uplifted above love and hate and storms of passion, calm amidst the eternal silences, fanned by zephyrs and bathed in living blue, peace rested for that one bright day on the Peak, as if it were some region

Where falls not rain, or hail, or any snow,
Or ever wind blows loudly.

We placed our names, with the date of ascent, in a tin

within a crevice, and descended to the Ledge, sitting on the smooth granite, getting our feet into cracks and against projections, and letting ourselves down by our hands, "Jim" going before me, so that I might steady my feet against his powerful shoulders. I was no longer giddy, and faced the precipice of 3,500 feet without a shiver. Repassing the Ledge and Lift, we accomplished the descent through 1,500 feet of ice and snow, with many falls and bruises, but no worse mishap, and there separated, the young men taking the steepest but most direct way to the "Notch," with the intention of getting ready for the march home, and "Jim" and I taking what he thought the safer route for me—a descent over boulders for 2,000 feet, and then a tremendous ascent to the "Notch." I had various falls, and once hung by my frock, which caught on a rock, and "Jim" severed it with his hunting knife, upon which I fell into a crevice full of soft snow. We were driven lower down the mountains than he had intended by impassable tracts of ice, and the ascent was tremendous. For the last 200 feet the boulders were of enormous size, and the steepness fearful. Sometimes I drew myself up on hands and knees, sometimes crawled; sometimes "Jim" pulled me up by my arms or a lariat, and sometimes I stood on his shoulders, or he made steps for me of his feet and hands, but at six we stood on the "Notch" in the splendor of the sinking sun, all color deepening, all peaks glorifying, all shadows purpling, all peril past.

"Jim" had parted with his *brusquerie* when we parted from the students, and was gentle and considerate beyond anything, though I knew that he must be grievously disappointed, both in my courage and strength. Water was an object of earnest desire. My tongue rattled in my mouth, and I could hardly articulate. It is good for one's sympathies to have for once a severe experience of thirst. Truly, there was

> *Water, water, everywhere,*
> *But not a drop to drink.*

Three times its apparent gleam deceived even the mountaineer's practised eye, but we found only a foot of "glare ice." At last, in a deep hole, he succeeded in breaking the ice, and by putting one's arm far down one could scoop up a little water in one's hand, but it was tormentingly insufficient. With great difficulty and much assistance I recrossed the "Lava Beds," was carried to the horse and lifted upon him, and when we reached the camping ground I was lifted off him, and laid on the ground wrapped up in blankets, a humiliating termination of a great exploit. The horses were saddled, and the young men were all ready to start, but "Jim" quietly said, "Now, gentlemen, I want a good night's rest, and we shan't stir from here to-night." I believe they were really glad to have it so, as one of them was quite "finished." I retired to my arbor, wrapped myself in a roll of blankets, and was soon asleep.

When I woke, the moon was high shining through the silvery branches, whitening the bald Peak above, and glittering on the great abyss of snow behind, and pine logs were blazing like a bonfire in the cold still air. My feet were so icy cold that I could not sleep again, and getting some blankets to sit in, and making a roll of them for my back, I sat for two hours by the camp-fire. It was weird and gloriously beautiful. The students were asleep not far off in their blankets with their feet towards the fire.

"Ring" lay on one side of me with his fine head on my arm, and his master sat smoking, with the fire lighting up the handsome side of his face, and except for the tones of our voices, and an occasional crackle and splutter as a pine knot blazed up, there was no sound on the mountain side. The beloved stars of my far-off home were overhead, the Plough and Pole Star, with their steady light; the glittering Pleiades, looking larger than I ever saw them, and "Orion's studded belt" shining gloriously. Once only some wild animals prowled near the camp, when "Ring," with one bound, disappeared from my side; and the horses, which were picketed by the stream, broke their lariats, stampeded, and came rushing wildly towards the fire, and it was fully half an hour before they were caught and quiet was restored. "Jim," or Mr. Nugent, as I always scrupulously called him, told stories of his early youth, and of a great sorrow which had led him to embark on a lawless and desperate life. His voice trembled, and tears rolled down his cheek. Was it semi-conscious acting, I wondered, or was his dark soul really stirred to its depths by the silence, the beauty, and the memories of youth?

We reached Estes Park at noon of the following day. A more successful ascent of the Peak was never made, and I would not now exchange my memories of its perfect beauty and extraordinary sublimity for any other experience of mountaineering in any part of the world. Yesterday snow fell on the summit, and it will be inaccessible for eight months to come.

I. L. B.

Letter VIII

✳

✢✤✦✢✤✦✢✤✦✢✤✦✢✤✦✢✤✦✢✤✦✢✤✦✢✤✦✢✤✦✢✤✦✢✤✦✢

ESTES PARK—BIG GAME—"PARKS" IN COLORADO—MAG-
NIFICENT SCENERY—FLOWERS AND PINES—AN AWFUL
ROAD—OUR LOG CABIN—GRIFFITH EVANS—A MINIA-
TURE WORLD—OUR TOPICS—A NIGHT ALARM—A SKUNK
—MORNING GLORIES—DAILY ROUTINE—THE PANIC—
"WAIT FOR THE WAGON"—A MUSICAL EVENING.

✢✤✦✢✤✦✢✤✦✢✤✦✢✤✦✢✤✦✢✤✦✢✤✦✢✤✦✢✤✦✢✤✦✢✤✦✢

ESTES PARK, COLORADO TERRITORY, *October 2.*

How time has slipped by I do not know. This is a glorious
region, and the air and life are intoxicating. I live mainly
out of doors and on horseback, wear my half-threadbare
Hawaiian dress, sleep sometimes under the stars on a bed
of pine boughs, ride on a Mexican saddle, and hear once
more the low music of my Mexican spurs. "There's a
stranger! Heave arf a brick at him!" is said by many travelers to express the feeling of the new settlers in these
Territories. This is not my experience in my cheery mountain home. How the rafters ring as I write with songs and
mirth, while the pitch-pine logs blaze and crackle in the
chimney, and the fine snow dust drives in through the
chinks and forms mimic snow wreaths on the floor, and
the wind raves and howls and plays among the creaking
pine branches and snaps them short off, and the lightning
plays round the blasted top of Long's Peak, and the hardy
hunters divert themselves with the thought that when I
go to bed I must turn out and face the storm!

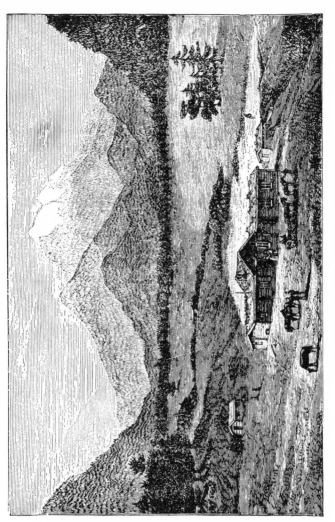

MY HOME IN THE ROCKY MOUNTAINS

You will ask, "What is Estes Park?" This name, with the quiet Midland Countries' sound, suggests "park palings" well lichened, a lodge with a curtseying woman, fallow deer, and a Queen Anne mansion. Such as it is, Estes Park is mine. It is unsurveyed, "no man's land," and mine by right of love, appropriation, and appreciation; by the seizure of its peerless sunrises and sunsets, its glorious afterglow, its blazing noons, its hurricanes sharp and furious, its wild auroras, its glories of mountain and forest, of canyon, lake, and river, and the stereotyping them all in my memory. Mine, too, in a better than the sportsman's sense, are its majestic wapiti, which play and fight under the pines in the early morning, as securely as fallow deer under our English oaks; its graceful "black-tails," swift of foot; its superb bighorns, whose noble leader is to be seen now and then with his classic head against the blue sky on the top of a colossal rock; its sneaking mountain lion with his hideous nocturnal caterwaulings, the great "grizzly," the beautiful skunk, the wary beaver, who is always making lakes, damming and turning streams, cutting down young cotton-woods, and setting an example of thrift and industry; the wolf, greedy and cowardly; the coyote and the lynx, and all the lesser fry of mink, marten, cat, hare, fox, squirrel, and chipmonk, as well as things that fly, from the eagle down to the crested blue-jay. May their number never be less, in spite of the hunter who kills for food and gain, and the sportsman who kills and marauds for pastime!

But still I have not answered the natural question,[1]

[1] Nor should I at this time, had not Henry Kingsley, Lord Dunraven, and "The Field," divulged the charms and whereabouts of

"What is Estes Park?" Among the striking peculiarities of these mountains are hundreds of high-lying valleys, large and small, at heights varying from 6,000 to 11,000 feet. The most important are North Park, held by hostile Indians; Middle Park, famous for hot springs and trout; South Park is 10,000 feet high, a great rolling prairie seventy miles long, well grassed and watered, but nearly closed by snow in winter. But parks innumerable are scattered throughout the mountains, most of them unnamed, and others nicknamed by the hunters or trappers who have made them their temporary resorts. They always lie far within the flaming Foot Hills, their exquisite stretches of flowery pastures dotted artistically with clumps of trees sloping lawnlike to bright swift streams full of red-waist-coated trout, or running up in soft glades into the dark forest, above which the snow peaks rise in their infinite majesty. Some are bits of meadow a mile long and very narrow, with a small stream, a beaver dam, and a pond made by beaver industry. Hundreds of these can only be reached by riding in the bed of a stream, or by scrambling up some narrow canyon till it debouches on the fairy-like stretch above. These parks are the feeding grounds of innumerable wild animals, and some, like one three miles off, seem chosen for the process of antler-casting, the grass being covered for at least a square mile with the magnificent branching horns of the elk.

Estes Park combines the beauties of all. Dismiss all thoughts of the Midland Counties. For park palings there are mountains, forest skirted, 9,000, 11,000, 14,000 feet high; for a lodge, two sentinel peaks of granite guarding

these "happy hunting grounds," with the certain result of directing a stream of tourists into the solitary, beast-haunted paradise.

the only feasible entrance; and for a Queen Anne mansion an unchinked log cabin with a vault of sunny blue overhead. The park is most irregularly shaped, and contains hardly any level grass. It is an aggregate of lawns, slopes, and glades, about eighteen miles in length, but never more than two miles in width. The Big Thompson, a bright, rapid trout stream, snow born on Long's Peak a few miles higher, takes all sorts of magical twists, vanishing and reappearing unexpectedly, glancing among lawns, rushing through romantic ravines, everywhere making music through the still, long nights. Here and there the lawns are so smooth, the trees so artistically grouped, a lake makes such an artistic foreground, or a waterfall comes tumbling down with such an apparent feeling for the picturesque, that I am almost angry with Nature for her close imitation of art. But in another hundred yards Nature, glorious, unapproachable, inimitable, is herself again, raising one's thoughts reverently upwards to her Creator and ours. Grandeur and sublimity, not softness, are the features of Estes Park. The glades which begin so softly are soon lost in the dark primæval forests, with their peaks of rosy granite, and their stretches of granite blocks piled and poised by nature in some mood of fury. The streams are lost in canyons nearly or quite inaccessible, awful in their blackness and darkness; every valley ends in mystery; seven mountain ranges raise their frowning barriers between us and the Plains, and at the south end of the park Long's Peak rises to a height of 14,700 feet, with his bare, scathed head slashed with eternal snow. The lowest part of the Park is 7,500 feet high; and though the sun is hot during the day, the mercury hovers near the freezing point every night of the summer. An immense quantity of snow falls, but partly owing to the tremendous winds which drift it into the deep valleys, and partly to the bright warm sun of the winter months, the park is never snowed up, and a number of cattle and horses are wintered out of doors on its sun-cured saccharine grasses, of which the *gramma* grass is the most valuable.

The soil here, as elsewhere in the neighborhood, is nearly everywhere coarse, grey, granitic dust, produced probably by the disintegration of the surrounding mountains. It does not hold water, and is never wet in any weather. There are no thaws here. The snow mysteriously disappears by rapid evaporation. Oats grow, but do not ripen, and, when well advanced, are cut and stacked for winter fodder. Potatoes yield abundantly, and, though not very large, are of the best quality, mealy throughout. Evans has not attempted anything else, and probably the more succulent vegetables would require irrigation. The wild flowers are gorgeous and innumerable, though their beauty, which culminates in July and August, was over before I arrived, and the recent snow flurries have finished them. The time between winter and winter is very short, and the flowery growth and blossom of a whole year are compressed into two months. Here are dandelions, buttercups, larkspurs, harebells, violets, roses, blue gentian, columbine, painter's brush, and fifty others, blue and yellow predominating; and though their blossoms are stiffened by the cold every morning, they are starring the grass and drooping over the brook long before noon, making the most of their brief lives in the sunshine. Of ferns, after many a long hunt, I have only found the *Cystopteris fragilis* and the *Blechnum spicant*, but I hear that the *Pteris aquilina* is also found. Snakes and mosquitoes do not appear to be known here. Coming almost direct from the tropics, one is dissatisfied with the uniformity of the foliage; indeed, foliage can hardly be written of, as the trees properly so called at this height are exclusively Coniferae, and bear needles instead of leaves. In places there are patches of spindly aspens, which have turned a lemon yellow, and along the streams bear cherries, vines, and roses lighten the gulches with their variegated crimson leaves. The pines are not imposing, either from their girth or height. Their coloring is blackish green, and though they are effective singly or in groups, they are somber and almost funereal when densely massed, as here, along the mountain sides. The timber line is at a height of about 11,000 feet, and is singularly well defined. The most attractive tree I have seen is the silver spruce, *Abies Englemanii*, near of kin to what is often called the balsam fir. Its shape and color are both beautiful. My heart warms towards it, and I frequent all the places where I can find it. It looks as if a soft, blue, silver powder had fallen on its deep-green needles, or as if a bluish hoar-frost, which must melt at noon, were resting upon it. Anyhow, one can hardly believe that the beauty is permanent, and survives the summer heat and the winter cold. The universal tree here is the *Pinus ponderosa*, but it never attains any very considerable size, and there is nothing to compare with the red-woods of the Sierra Nevada, far less with the sequoias of California.

As I have written before, Estes Park is thirty miles from Longmount, the nearest settlement, and it can be reached on horseback only by the steep and devious track by which I came, passing through a narrow rift in the top of a precipitous ridge, 9,000 feet high, called the Devil's Gate.

Evans takes a lumber wagon with four horses over the mountains, and a Colorado engineer would have no difficulty in making a wagon road. In several of the gulches over which the track hangs there are the remains of wagons which have come to grief in the attempt to emulate Evans's feat, which without evidence, I should have supposed to be impossible. It is an awful road. The only settlers in the park are Griffith Evans, and a married man a mile higher up. "Mountain Jim's" cabin is in the entrance gulch, four miles off, and there is not another cabin for eighteen miles toward the Plains. The park is unsurveyed, and the huge tract of mountainous country beyond is almost altogether unexplored. Elk hunters occasionally come up and camp out here; but the two settlers, who, however, are only squatters, for various reasons are not disposed to encourage such visitors. When Evans, who is a very successful hunter, came here, he came on foot, and for some time after settling here he carried the flour and necessaries required by his family on his back over the mountains.

As I intend to make Estes Park my headquarters until the winter sets in, I must make you acquainted with my surroundings and mode of living. The "Queen Anne mansion" is represented by a log cabin made of big hewn logs. The chinks should be filled with mud and lime, but these are wanting. The roof is formed of barked young spruce, then a layer of hay, and an outer coating of mud, all nearly flat. The floors are roughly boarded. The "living room" is about sixteen feet square, and has a rough stone chimney in which pine logs are always burning. At one end there is a door into a small bedroom, and at the other a door into a small eating room, at the table of which we feed in relays.

This opens into a very small kitchen with a great American cooking-stove, and there are two "bed closets" besides. Although rude, it is comfortable, except for the draughts. The fine snow drives in through the chinks and covers the floors, but sweeping it out at intervals is both fun and exercise. There are no heaps or rubbish places outside. Near it, on the slope under the pines, is a pretty two-roomed cabin, and beyond that, near the lake, is my cabin, a very rough one. My door opens into a little room with a stone chimney, and that again into a small room with a hay bed, a chair with a tin basin on it, a shelf and some pegs. A small window looks on the lake, and the glories of the sunrises which I see from it are indescribable. Neither of my doors has a lock, and, to say the truth, neither will shut, as the wood has swelled. Below the house, on the stream which issues from the lake, there is a beautiful log dairy, with a water wheel outside, used for churning. Besides this, there are a *corral,* a shed for the wagon, a room for the hired man, and shelters for horses and weakly calves. All these things are necessaries at this height.

The ranchmen are two Welshmen, Evans and Edwards, each with a wife and family. The men are as diverse as they can be. "Griff," as Evans is called, is short and small, and is hospitable, careless, reckless, jolly, social, convivial, peppery, good natured, "nobody's enemy but his own." He had the wit and taste to find out Estes Park, where people have found him out, and have induced him to give them food and lodging, and add cabin to cabin to take them in. He is a splendid shot, an expert and successful hunter, a bold mountaineer, a good rider, a capital cook, and a generally "jolly fellow." His cheery laugh rings through the cabin from the early morning, and is contagious, and when the rafters ring at night with such songs as "D'ye ken John Peel?" "Auld Lang Syne," and "John Brown," what would the chorus be without poor "Griff's" voice? What would Estes Park be without him, indeed? When he went to Denver lately we missed him as we should have missed the sunshine, and perhaps more. In the early morning, when Long's Peak is red, and the grass crackles with the hoar-frost, he arouses me with a cheery thump on my door. "We're going cattle-hunting, will you come?" or, "Will you help to drive in the cattle? You can take your pick of the horses. I want another hand." Free-hearted, lavish, popular, poor "Griff" loves liquor too well for his prosperity, and is always tormented by debt. He makes lots of money, but puts it into "a bag with holes." He has fifty horses and 1,000 head of cattle, many of which are his own, wintering up here, and makes no end of money by taking in people at eight dollars a week, yet it all goes somehow. He has a most industrious wife, a girl of seventeen, and four younger children, all musical, but the wife has to work like a slave; and though he is a kind husband, her lot, as compared with her lord's, is like that of a squaw. Edwards, his partner, is his exact opposite, tall, thin, and condemnatory looking, keen, industrious, saving, grave, a teetotaler, grieved for all reasons at Evans's follies, and rather grudging; as naturally unpopular as Evans is popular; a "decent man," who, with his industrious wife, will certainly make money as fast as Evans loses it.

I pay eight dollars a week, which includes the unlimited use of a horse, when one can be found and caught. We breakfast at seven on beef, potatoes, tea, coffee, new bread, and butter. Two pitchers of cream and two of milk are replenished as fast as they are exhausted. Dinner at twelve is a repetition of the breakfast, but with the coffee omitted and a gigantic pudding added. Tea at six is a repetition of breakfast. "Eat whenever you are hungry, you can always get milk and bread in the kitchen," Evans says—"eat as much as you can, it'll do you good"—and we all eat like hunters. There is no change of food. The steer which was being killed on my arrival is now being eaten through from head to tail, the meat being hacked off quite promiscuously, without any regard to joints. In this dry, rarefied air, the outside of the flesh blackens and hardens, and though the weather may be hot, the carcass keeps sweet for two or three months. The bread is super excellent, but the poor wives seem to be making and baking it all day.

The regular household living and eating together at this time consists of a very intelligent and high-minded American couple, Mr. and Mrs. Dewy, people whose character, culture, and society I should value anywhere; a young Englishman, brother of a celebrated African traveler, who, because he rides on an English saddle, and clings to some other insular peculiarities, is called "The Earl"; a miner prospecting for silver; a young man, the type of intelligent, practical "Young America," whose health showed consumptive tendencies when he was in business, and who is living a hunter's life here; a grown-up niece of Evans; and a melancholy-looking hired man. A mile off there is an industrious married settler, and four miles off, in the gulch leading to the park, "Mountain Jim," otherwise Mr. Nugent, is posted. His business as a trapper takes him daily up to the beaver dams in Black Canyon to look after his traps, and he generally spends some time in or about our cabin, not, I can see, to Evans's satisfaction. For, in truth, this blue hollow, lying solitary at the foot of Long's Peak, is a miniature world of great interest, in which love, jealousy, hatred, envy, pride, unselfishness, greed, selfishness, and self-sacrifice can be studied hourly, and there is always the unpleasantly exciting risk of an open quarrel with the neighboring desperado, whose "I'll shoot you!" has more than once been heard in the cabin.

The party, however, has often been increased by "campers," either elk hunters or "prospectors" for silver or locations, who feed with us and join us in the evening. They get little help from Evans, either as to elk or locations, and go away disgusted and unsuccessful. Two Englishmen of refinement and culture camped out here prospecting a few weeks ago, and then, contrary to advice, crossed the mountains into North Park, where gold is said to abound, and it is believed that they have fallen victims to the bloodthirsty Indians of the region. Of course, we never get letters or newspapers unless some one rides to Longmount for them. Two or three novels and a copy of *Our New West* are our literature. Our latest newspaper is seventeen days old. Somehow the park seems to become the natural limit of our interests so far as they appear in conversation at table. The last grand aurora, the prospect of a snow-storm, track and sign of elk and grizzly, rumors of a bighorn herd near the lake, the canyons in which the Texan cattle were last seen, the merits of different rifles, the progress of two obvious love affairs, the probability of some one coming up from the Plains with letters, "Mountain Jim's" latest mood or escapade, and the merits of his dog "Ring" as compared with those of Evans's dog

"Plunk," are among the topics which are never abandoned as exhausted.

On Sunday work is nominally laid aside, but most of the men go out hunting or fishing till the evening, when we have the harmonium and much sacred music and singing in parts. To be alone in the park from the afternoon till the last glory of the afterglow has faded, with no books but a Bible and Prayer-book, is truly delightful. No worthier temple for a "Te Deum" or "Gloria in Excelsis" could be found than this "temple not made with hands," in which one may worship without being distracted by the sight of bonnets of endless form, and curiously intricate "back hair," and countless oddities of changing fashion.

I shall not soon forget my first night here.

Somewhat dazed by the rarefied air, entranced by the glorious beauty, slightly puzzled by the motley company, whose faces loomed not always quite distinctly through the cloud of smoke produced by eleven pipes, I went to my solitary cabin at nine, attended by Evans. It was very dark, and it seemed a long way off. Something howled—Evans said it was a wolf—and owls apparently innumerable hooted incessantly. The pole-star, exactly opposite my cabin door, burned like a lamp. The frost was sharp. Evans opened the door, lighted a candle, and left me, and I was soon in my hay bed. I was frightened—that is, afraid of being frightened, it was so eerie—but sleep soon got the better of my fears. I was awoke by a heavy breathing, a noise something like sawing under the floor, and a pushing and upheaving, all very loud. My candle was all burned, and, in truth, I dared not stir. The noise went on for an hour fully, when, just as I thought the floor had been made sufficiently thin for all purposes of ingress, the sounds abruptly ceased, and I fell asleep again. My hair was not, as it ought to have been, white in the morning!

I was dressed by seven, our breakfast hour, and when I reached the great cabin and told my story, Evans laughed hilariously, and Edwards contorted his face dismally. They told me that there was a skunk's lair under my cabin, and that they dare not make any attempt to dislodge him for fear of rendering the cabin untenable. They have tried to trap him since, but without success, and each night the noisy performance is repeated. I think he is sharpening his claws on the under side of my floor, as the grizzlies sharpen theirs upon the trees. The odor with which this creature, truly named Mephitis, can overpower its assailants is truly *awful*. We were driven out of the cabin for some hours merely by the passage of one across the *corral*. The bravest man is a coward in its neighborhood. Dogs rub their noses on the ground till they bleed when they have touched the fluid, and even die of the vomiting produced by the effluvia. The odor can be smelt a mile off. If clothes are touched by the fluid they must be destroyed. At present its fur is very valuable. Several have been killed since I came. A shot well aimed at the spine secures one safely, and an experienced dog can kill one by leaping upon it suddenly without being exposed to danger. It is a beautiful beast, about the size and length of a fox, with long thick black or dark-brown fur, and two white streaks from the head to the long bushy tail. The claws of its fore-feet are long and polished. Yesterday one was seen rushing from the dairy and was shot. "Plunk," the big dog, touched it and has to be driven into exile. The body was valiantly removed by a man with a long fork, and carried to a running stream, but we are nearly choked with the odor from the spot where it fell. I hope that my skunk will enjoy a quiet spirit so long as we are near neighbors.

October 3.

This is surely one of the most entrancing spots on earth. Oh, that I could paint with pen or brush! From my bed I look on Mirror Lake, and with the very earliest dawn, when objects are not discernible, it lies there absolutely still, a purplish lead color. Then suddenly into its mirror flash inverted peaks, at first a bright orange, then changing into red, making the dawn darker all round. This is a new sight, each morning new. Then the peaks fade, and when morning is no longer "spread upon the mountains," the pines are mirrored in my lake almost as solid objects, and the glory steals downwards, and a red flush warms the clear atmosphere of the park, and the hoar-frost sparkles and the crested blue-jays step forth daintily on the jewelled grass. The majesty and beauty grow on me daily. As I crossed from my cabin just now, and the long mountain shadows lay on the grass, and form and color gained new meanings, I was almost false to Hawaii; I couldn't go on writing for the glory of the sunset, but went out and sat on a rock to see the deepening blue in the dark canyons, and the peaks becoming rose color one by one, then fading into sudden ghastliness, the awe-inspiring heights of Long's Peak fading last. Then came the glories of the afterglow, when the orange and lemon of the east faded into gray, and then gradually the gray for some distance above the horizon brightened into a cold blue, and above the blue into a broad band of rich, warm red, with an

ESTES PARK

upper band of rose color; above it hung a big cold moon. This is the "daily miracle" of evening, as the blazing peaks in the darkness of Mirror Lake are the miracle of morning. Perhaps this scenery is not lovable, but, as if it were a strong stormy character, it has an intense fascination.

The routine of my day is breakfast at seven, then I go back and "do" my cabin and draw water from the lake, read a little, loaf a little, return to the big cabin and sweep it alternately with Mrs. Dewy, after which she reads aloud till dinner at twelve. Then I ride with Mr. Dewy, or by myself, or with Mrs. Dewy, who is learning to ride cavalier fashion in order to accompany her invalid husband, or go after cattle till supper at six. After that we all sit in the living room, and I settle down to write to you, or mend my clothes, which are dropping to pieces. Some sit round the table playing at eucre, the strange hunters and prospectors lie on the floor smoking, and rifles are cleaned, bullets cast, fishing flies made, fishing tackle repaired, boots are waterproofed, part-songs are sung, and about half-past eight I cross the crisp grass to my cabin, always expecting to find something in it. We all wash our own clothes, and as my stock is so small, some part of every day has to be spent at the wash tub. Politeness and propriety always prevail in our mixed company, and though various grades of society are represented, true democratic equality prevails, not its counterfeit, and there is neither forwardness on one side nor condescension on the other.

Evans left for Denver ten days ago, taking his wife and family to the Plains for the winter, and the mirth of our party departed with him. Edwards is somber, except when he lies on the floor in the evening, and tells stories of his march through Georgia with Sherman. I gave Evans a

100-dollar note to change, and asked him to buy me a horse for my tour, and for three days we have expected him. The mail depends on him. I have had no letters from you for five weeks, and can hardly curb my impatience. I ride or walk three or four miles out on the Longmount trail two or three times a day to look for him. Others, for different reasons, are nearly equally anxious. After dark we start at every sound, and every time the dogs bark all the able-bodied of us turn out *en masse.* "Wait for the wagon" has become a nearly maddening joke.

October 9.

The letter and newspaper fever has seized on every one. We have sent at last to Longmount. The evening I rode out on the Longmount trail towards dusk, escorted by "Mountain Jim," and in the distance we saw a wagon with four horses and a saddle horse behind, and the driver waved a handkerchief, the concerted signal if I were the possessor of a horse. We turned back, galloping down the long hill as fast as two good horses could carry us, and gave the joyful news. It was an hour before the wagon arrived, bringing not Evans but two "campers" of suspicious aspect, who have pitched their camp close to my cabin! You cannot imagine what it is to be locked in by these mountain walls, and not to know where your letters are lying. Later on, Mr. Buchan, one of our usual inmates, returned from Denver with papers, letters for every one but me, and much exciting news. The financial panic has spread out West, gathering strength on its way. The Denver banks have all suspended business. They refuse to cash their own checks, or to allow their customers to draw a dollar, and would not even give greenbacks for my English gold! Neither Mr. Buchan nor Evans could get a cent. Business is suspended, and everybody, however rich, is for the time being poor. The Indians have taken to the "war path," and are burning ranches and killing cattle. There is a regular "scare" among the settlers, and wagon loads of fugitives are arriving in Colorado Springs. The Indians say, "The white man has killed the buffalo and left them to rot on the plains. We will be revenged." Evans had reached Longmount, and will be here tonight.

October 10

"Wait for the wagon" still! We had a hurricane of wind and hail last night; it was eleven before I could go to my cabin, and I only reached it with the help of two men. The moon was not up, and the sky overhead was black with clouds, when suddenly Long's Peak, which had been invisible, gleamed above the dark mountains, all glistening with new-fallen snow, on which the moon, as yet unrisen here, was shining. The evening before, after sunset, I saw another novel effect. My lake turned a brilliant orange in the twilight, and in its still mirror the mountains were reflected a deep rich blue. It is a world of wonders. To-day we had a great storm with flurries of fine snow; and when the clouds rolled up at noon, the Snowy Range and all the higher mountains were pure white. I have been hard at work all day to drown my anxieties, which are heightened by a rumor that Evans has gone buffalo-hunting on the Platte!

This evening, quite unexpectedly, Evans arrived with a heavy mail in a box. I sorted it, but there was nothing for me, and Evans said he was afraid that he had left my letters, which were separate from the others, behind at Denver, but he had written from Longmount for them. A few hours later they were found in a box of groceries!

All the hilarity of the house has returned with Evans, and he has brought a kindred spirit with him, a young man who plays and sings splendidly, has an inexhaustible *repertoire*, and produces sonatas, funeral marches, anthems, reels, strathspeys, and all else, out of his wonderful memory. Never, surely was a chamber organ compelled to such service. A little cask of suspicious appearance was smuggled into the cabin from the wagon, and heightens the hilarity a little, I fear. No churlishness could resist Evans's unutterable jollity or the contagion of his hearty laugh. He claps people on the back, shouts at them, will do anything for them, and makes a perpetual breeze. "My kingdom for a horse!" He has not got one for me, and a shadow crossed his face when I spoke of the subject. Eventually he asked for a private conference, when he told me, with some confusion, that he had found himself "very hard up" in Denver, and had been obliged to appropriate my 100-dollar note. He said he would give me, as interest for it up to November 25th, a good horse, saddle, and bridle for my proposed journey of 600 miles. I was somewhat dismayed, but there was no other course, as the money was gone.[2] I tried a horse, mended my clothes, reduced my pack to a weight of twelve pounds, and was all ready for an early start, when before daylight I was wakened by Evans's cheery voice at my door. "I say, Miss B., we've got to drive

[2] In justice to Evans, I must mention here that every cent of the money was ultimately paid, that the horse was perfection, and that the arrangement turned out a most advantageous one for me.

wild cattle to-day; I wish you' lend a hand, there's not enough of us; I'll give you a good horse; one day won't make much difference." So we've been driving cattle all day, riding about twenty miles, and fording the Big Thompson about as many times. Evans flatters me by saying that I am "as much use as another man"; more than one of our party, I hope, who always avoided the "ugly" cows.

October 12.

I am still here, helping in the kitchen, driving cattle, and riding four or five times a day. Evans detains me each morning by saying, "Here's lots of horses for you to try," and after trying five or six a day, I do not find one to my liking. Today, as I was cantering a tall well-bred one round the lake, he threw the bridle off by a toss of his head, leaving me with the reins in my hands; one bucked, and two have tender feet, and tumbled down. Such are some of our little varieties. Still I hope to get off on my tour in a day or two, so at least as to be able to compare Estes Park with some of the better-known parts of Colorado.

You would be amused if you could see our cabin just now. There are nine men in the room and three women. For want of seats most of the men are lying on the floor; all are smoking, and the blithe young French Canadian who plays so beautifully, and catches about fifty speckled trout for each meal, is playing the harmonium with a pipe in his mouth. Three men who have camped in Black Canyon for a week are lying like dogs on the floor. They are all over six feet high, immovably solemn, neither smiling at the general hilarity, nor at the absurd changes which are being rung on the harmonium. They may be described as clothed only in boots, for their clothes are torn to rags. They stare vacantly. They have neither seen a woman nor slept under a roof for six months. Negro songs are being sung, and before that "Yankee Doodle" was played immediately after "Rule Britannia," and it made every one but the strangers laugh, it sounded so foolish and mean. The colder weather is bringing the beasts down from the heights. I heard both wolves and the mountain lion as I crossed to my cabin last night.

I. L. B.

Letter IX

*

+⚘+✳+⚘+✳+⚘+✳+⚘+✳+⚘+✳+⚘+✳+⚘+✳+⚘+✳+⚘+✳+⚘+✳+⚘+✳+⚘

"Please Ma'ams"—A desperado—A cattle hunt—
The muster—A mad cow—A snow-storm—Snowed
up—Birdie—The Plains—A prairie schooner—Denver—A find—Plum Creek—"Being agreeable"—
Snowbound—The grey mare.

+⚘+✳+⚘+✳+⚘+✳+⚘+✳+⚘+✳+⚘+✳+⚘+✳+⚘+✳+⚘+✳+⚘+✳+⚘+✳+⚘

Estes Park, Colorado.

This afternoon, as I was reading in my cabin, little Sam
Edwards ran in, saying, "Mountain Jim wants to speak to
you." This brought to my mind images of infinite worry,
gauche servants, "please Ma'ams," *contretemps*, and the
habit growing out of our elaborate and uselessly conventional life of magnifying the importance of similar trifles.
Then "things" came up, with the tyranny they exercise.
I *really* need nothing more than this log cabin offers. But
elsewhere one must have a house and servants, and burdens
and worries—not that one may be hospitable and comfortable, but for the "thick clay" in the shape of "things"
which one has accumulated. My log house takes me about
five minutes to "do," and you could eat off the floor, and
it needs no lock, as it contains nothing worth stealing.

But "Mountain Jim" was waiting while I made these
reflections to ask us to take a ride; and he, Mr. and Mrs.
Dewy, and I, had a delightful stroll through colored foliage, and then, when they were fatigued, I changed my
horse for his beautiful mare, and we galloped and raced in

the beautiful twilight, in the intoxicating frosty air. Mrs. Dewy wishes you could have seen us as we galloped down the pass, the fearful-looking ruffian on my heavy wagon horse, and I on his bare wooden saddle, from which beaver, mink, and marten tails, and pieces of skin, were hanging raggedly, with one spur, and feet not in the stirrups, the mare looking so aristocratic and I so beggarly! Mr. Nugent is what is called "splendid company." With a sort of breezy mountain recklessness in everything, he passes remarkably acute judgments on men and events; on women also. He has pathos, poetry, and humor, an intense love of nature, strong vanity in certain directions, an obvious desire to act and speak in character, and sustain his reputation as a desperado, a considerable acquaintance with literature, a wonderful verbal memory, opinions on every person and subject, a chivalrous respect for women in his manner, which makes it all the more amusing when he suddenly turns round upon one with some graceful raillery, a great power of fascination, and a singular love of children. The children of this house run to him, and when he sits down they climb on his broad shoulders and play with his curls. They say in the house that "no one who has been here thinks any one worth speaking to after Jim," but I think that this is probably an opinion which time would alter. Somehow, he is kept always before the public of Colorado, for one can hardly take up a newspaper without finding a paragraph about him, a contribution by him, or a fragment of his biography. Ruffian as he looks, the first word he speaks—to a lady, at least—places him on a level with educated gentlemen, and his conversation is brilliant, and full of the light and fitfulness of genius. Yet, on the whole, he is a most painful spectacle.

His magnificent head shows so plainly the better possibilities which might have been his. His life, in spite of a certain dazzle which belongs to it, is a ruined and wasted one, and one asks what of good can the future have in store for one who has for so long chosen evil?[1]

Shall I ever get away? We were to have had a grand cattle hunt yesterday, beginning at 6:30, but the horses were all lost. Often out of fifty horses all that are worth anything are marauding, and a day is lost in hunting for them in the canyons. However, before daylight this morning Evans called through my door, "Miss Bird, I say we've got to drive cattle fifteen miles, I wish you'd lend a hand; there's not enough of us; I'll give you a good horse."

The scene of the drive is at a height of 7,500 feet, watered by two rapid rivers. On all sides mountains rise to an altitude of from 11,000 to 15,000 feet, their skirts shaggy with pitch-pine forests, and scarred by deep canyons, wooded and boulder strewn, opening upon the mountain pasture previously mentioned. Two thousand head of half-wild Texan cattle are scattered in herds throughout the canyons, living on more or less suspicious terms with grizzly and brown bears, mountain lions, elk, mountain sheep, spotted deer, wolves, lynxes, wild cats, beavers, minks, skunks, chipmonks, eagles, rattlesnakes, and all the other two-legged, four-legged, vertebrate, and invertebrate inhabitants of this lonely and romantic region. On the whole, they show a tendency rather to the habits of wild than of domestic cattle. They march to water in Indian file, with the bulls leading, and when threatened, take strategic advantage of ridgy ground, slinking warily along in the

[1] September of the next year answered the question by laying him down in a dishonored grave, with a rifle bullet in his brain.

hollows, the bulls acting as sentinels, and bringing up the rear in case of an attack from dogs. Cows have to be regularly broken in for milking, being as wild as buffaloes in their unbroken state; but, owing to the comparative dryness of the grasses, and the system of allowing the calf to have the milk during the daytime, a dairy of 200 cows does not produce as much butter as a Devonshire dairy of fifty. Some "necessary" cruelty is involved in the stockman's business, however humane he may be. The system is one of terrorism, and from the time that the calf is bullied into the branding pen, and the hot iron burns into his shrinking flesh, to the day when the fatted ox is driven down from his boundless pastures to be slaughtered in Chicago, "the fear and dread of man" are upon him.

The herds are apt to penetrate the savage canyons which come down from the Snowy Range, when they incur a risk of being snowed up and starved, and it is necessary now and then to hunt them out and drive them down to the "park." On this occasion, the whole were driven down for a muster, and for the purpose of branding the calves.

After a 6:30 breakfast this morning, we started, the party being composed of my host, a hunter from the Snowy Range, two stockmen from the Plains, one of whom rode a violent buck-jumper, and was said by his comrade to be the "best rider in North Americay," and myself. We were all mounted on Mexican saddles, rode, as the custom is, with light snaffle bridles, leather guards over our feet, and broad wooden stirrups, and each carried his lunch in a pouch slung on the lassoing horn of his saddle. Four big, badly-trained dogs accompanied us. It was a ride of nearly thirty miles, and of many hours, one of the most splendid I ever took. We never got off our horses except to tighten the girths, we ate our lunch with our bridles knotted over our saddle horns, started over the level at full gallops, leapt over trunks of trees, dashed madly down hillsides rugged with rocks or strewn with great stones, forded deep, rapid streams, saw lovely lakes and views of surpassing magnificence, startled a herd of elk with uncouth heads and in the chase, which for some time was unsuccessful, rode to the very base of Long's Peak, over 14,000 feet high, where the bright waters of one of the affluents of the Platte burst from the eternal snows through a canyon of indescribable majesty. The sun was hot, but at a height of over 8,000 feet the air was crisp and frosty, and the enjoyment of riding a good horse under such exhilarating circumstances was extreme. In one wild part of the ride we had to come down a steep hill, thickly wooded with pitch pines, to leap over the fallen timber, and steer between the dead and living trees to avoid being "snagged," or bringing down a heavy dead branch by an unwary touch.

Emerging from this, we caught sight of a thousand Texan cattle feeding in a valley below. The leaders scented us, and, taking fright, began to move off in the direction of the open "park," while we were about a mile from and above them. "Head them off, boys!" our leader shouted; "all aboard; hark away!" and with something of the "High, tally-ho in the morning!" away we all went at a hard gallop down-hill. I could not hold my excited animal; down-hill, up-hill, leaping over rocks and timber, faster every moment the pace grew, and still the leader shouted, "Go it, boys!" and the horses dashed on at racing speed, passing and repassing each other, till my small but beautiful bay was keeping pace with the immense strides of the great buck-jumper ridden by "the finest rider in North Americay," and I was dizzied and breathless by the pace at which we were going. A shorter time than it takes to tell it brought us close to and abreast of the surge of cattle. The bovine waves were a grand sight: huge bulls, shaped like buffaloes, bellowed and roared, and with great oxen and cows with yearling calves, galloped like racers, and we galloped alongside of them, and shortly headed them and in no time were placed as sentinels across the mouth of the valley. It seemed like infantry awaiting the shock of cavalry as we stood as still as our excited horses would allow. I almost quailed as the surge came on, but when it got close to us my comrades hooted fearfully, and we dashed forward with the dogs, and, with bellowing, roaring, and thunder of hoofs, the wave receded as it came. I rode up to our leader, who received me with much laughter. He said I was "a good cattleman," and that he had forgotten that a lady was of the party till he saw me "come leaping over the timber, and driving with the others."

It was not for two hours after this that the real business of driving began, and I was obliged to change my thoroughbred for a well-trained cattle horse—a *bronco*, which could double like a hare, and go over any ground. I had not expected to work like a *vachero*, but so it was, and my Hawaiian experience was very useful. We hunted the various canyons and known "camps," driving the herds out of them; and, until we had secured 850 head in the *corral* some hours afterwards, we scarcely saw each other to speak to. Our first difficulty was with a herd which got into some swampy ground, when a cow, which afterwards gave me an infinity of trouble, remained at bay for nearly an hour, tossing the dog three times, and resisting all efforts to dislodge her. She had a large yearling calf with her, and Evans told me that the attachment of a cow to her first calf is sometimes so great that she will kill her second that the first may have the milk. I got a herd of over a hundred out of a canyon by myself, and drove them down to the river with the aid of one badly-broken dog, which gave me more trouble than the cattle. The getting over was most troublesome; a few took to the water readily and went across, but others smelt it, and then, doubling back, ran in various directions; while some attacked the dog as he was swimming, and others, after crossing, headed back in search of some favorite companions which had been left behind, and one specially vicious cow attacked my horse over and over again. It took an hour and a half of time and much patience to gather them all on the other side.

It was getting late in the day, and a snowstorm was impending, before I was joined by the other drivers and herds, and as the former had diminished to three, with only three dogs, it was very difficult to keep the cattle together. You drive them as gently as possible, so as not to frighten or excite them,[2] riding first on one side, then on

[2] In several visits to America I have observed that the Americans are far in advance of us and our colonial kinsmen in their treatment of horses and other animals. This was very apparent with regard to this Texan herd. There were no stock whips, no needless worrying of the animals in the excitement of sport. Any dog seizing a bullock by his tail or heels would have been called off and punished, and quietness and gentleness were the rule. The horses were ridden without whips, and with spurs so blunt that they could not hurt even a human skin, and were ruled by the voice and a slight pressure on the light snaffle bridle. This is the usual plan, even where, as in Colorado, the horses are *bronchos*, and inherit ineradicable vice. I never yet saw a horse *bullied* into submission in the United States.

the other, to guide them; and if they deliberately go in a wrong direction, you gallop in front and head them off. The great excitement is when one breaks away from the herd and gallops madly up and down-hill, and you gallop after him anywhere, over and among rocks and trees, doubling when he doubles, and heading him till you get him back again. The bulls were quite easily managed, but the cows with calves, old or young, were most troublesome. By accident I rode between one cow and her calf in a narrow place, and the cow rushed at me and was just getting her big horns under the horse, when he reared, and spun dexterously aside. This kind of thing happened continually. There was one very handsome red cow which became quite mad. She had a calf with her nearly her own size, and thought every one its enemy, and though its horns were well developed, and it was quite able to take care of itself, she insisted on protecting it from all fancied dangers. One of the dogs, a young, foolish thing, seeing that the cow was excited, took a foolish pleasure in barking at her, and she was eventually quite infuriated. She turned to bay forty times at least; tore up the ground with her horns, tossed and killed the calves of two other cows, and finally became so dangerous to the rest of the herd that, just as the drive was ending, Evans drew his revolver and shot her, and the calf for which she had fought so blindly lamented her piteously. She rushed at me several times mad with rage, but these trained cattle horses keep perfectly cool, and, nearly without will on my part, mine jumped aside at the right moment, and foiled the assailant. Just at dusk we reached the corral—an acre of grass enclosed by stout post-and-rail fences seven feet high—and by much patience and some subtlety lodged the whole herd within its shelter, without a blow, a shout, or even a crack of a whip, wild as the cattle were. It was fearfully cold. We galloped the last mile and a half in four and a half minutes, reached the cabin just as the snow began to fall, and found strong, hot tea ready.

October 18.

Snow-bound for three days! I could not write yester-day, it was so awful. People gave up all occupation, and talked of nothing but the storm. The hunters all kept by the great fire in the living room, only going out to bring in logs and clear the snow from the door and windows. I never spent a more fearful night than two nights ago, alone in my cabin in the storm, with the roof lifting, the mud cracking and coming off, and the fine snow hissing through the chinks between the logs, while splittings and breaking of dead branches, wind wrung and snow laden, went on incessantly, with screechings, howlings, thunder and lightning, and many unfamiliar sounds besides. After snowing fiercely all day, another foot of it fell in the early night, and, after drifting against my door, blocked me effectually in. About midnight the mercury fell to zero, and soon after a gale rose, which lasted for ten hours. My window frame is swelled, and shuts, apparently, hermeti-cally; and my bed is six feet from it. I had gone to sleep with six blankets on, and a heavy sheet over my face. Be-tween two and three I was awoke by the cabin being shifted from underneath by the wind, and the sheet was frozen to my lips. I put out my hands, and the bed was thickly covered with fine snow. Getting up to investigate matters, I found the floor some inches deep in parts in fine snow, and a gust of fine, needle-like snow stung my face. The bucket of water was solid ice. I lay in bed freezing till sunrise, when some of the men came to see if I "was alive," and to dig me out. They brought a can of hot water, which turned to ice before I could use it. I dressed standing in snow, and my brushes, boots, and etceteras were covered with snow. When I ran to the house, not a mountain or anything else could be seen, and the snow on one side was drifted higher than the roof. The air, as high as one could see, was one white, stinging smoke of snow-drift—a terrific sight. In the living room, the snow was driving through the chinks, and Mrs. Dewy was shoveling it from the floor. Mr. D.'s beard was hoary with frost in a room with a fire all night. Evans was lying ill, with his bed covered with snow. Returning from my cabin after breakfast, loaded with occupations for the day, I was lifted off my feet, and deposited in a drift, and all my things, writing book and letter included, were carried in different directions. Some, including a valuable photograph, were irrecoverable. The writing book was found, some hours afterwards, under three feet of snow.

There are tracks of bears and deer close to the house, but no one can hunt in this gale, and the drift is blinding. We have been slightly overcrowded in our one room. Chess, music, and whist have been resorted to. One hunter, for very *ennui*, has devoted himself to keeping my ink from freezing. We all sat in great cloaks and coats, and kept up an enormous fire, with the pitch running out of the logs. The isolation is extreme, for we are literally snowed up, and the other settler in the Park and "Mountain Jim" are both at Denver. Late in the evening the storm ceased. In some places the ground is bare of snow, while in others all irregularities are leveled, and the drifts are forty feet deep. Nature is grand under this new aspect. The cold is awful; the high wind with the mercury at zero would skin any part exposed to it.

October 19.

Evans offers me six dollars a week if I will stay into the winter and do the cooking after Mrs. Edwards leaves! I think I should like playing at being a "hired girl" if it were not for the bread-making! But it would suit me better to ride after cattle. The men don't like "baching," as it is called in the wilds—i.e. "doing for themselves." They washed and ironed their clothes yesterday, and there was an incongruity about the last performance. I really think (though for the fifteenth time) that I shall leave to-morrow. The cold has moderated, the sky is bluer than ever, the snow is evaporating, and a hunter who has joined us to-day says that there are no drifts on the trail which one cannot get through.

LONGMOUNT, COLORADO, October 20.

"The Island Valley of Avillon" is left, but how shall I finally tear myself from its freedom and enchantments? I see Long's snowy peak rising into the night sky, and know and long after the magnificence of the blue hollow at its base. We were to have left at 8 but the horses were lost, so it was 9:30 before we started, the *we* being the musical young French Canadian and myself. I have a bay Indian pony, "Birdie," a little beauty, with legs of iron, fast, enduring, gentle, and wise; and with luggage for some weeks, including a black silk dress, behind my saddle, I am tolerably independent. It was a most glorious ride. We passed through the gates of rock, through gorges where the unsunned snow lay deep under the lemon-colored aspens; caught glimpses of far-off, snow-clad giants rising into a sky of deep sad blue; lunched above the Foot Hills at a cabin where two brothers and a "hired man" were "keeping bach," where everything was so trim, clean, and ornamental that one did not miss a woman; crossed a deep backwater on a narrow beaver dam, because the log bridge was broken down, and emerged from the brilliantly-colored canyon of the St. Vrain just at dusk upon the featureless prairies, when we had some trouble in finding Longmount in the dark. A hospitable welcome awaited me at this inn, and an English friend came in and spent the evening with me.

GREAT PLATTE CANYON, *October 23.*

My letters on this tour will, I fear, be very dull, for after riding all day, looking after my pony, getting supper, hearing about various routes, and the pastoral, agricultural, mining, and hunting gossip of the neighborhood, I am so sleepy and wholesomely tired that I can hardly write. I left Longmount pretty early on Tuesday morning, the day being sad, with the blink of an impending snow-storm in the air. The evening before I was introduced to a man who had been a colonel in the rebel army, who made a most unfavorable impression upon me, and it was a great annoyance to me when he presented himself on horse-back to guide me "over the most intricate part of the journey." Solitude is infinitely preferable to uncongeniality, and is bliss when compared with repulsiveness, so I was thoroughly glad when I got rid of my escort and set out upon the prairie alone. It is a dreary ride of thirty miles over the low brown plains to Denver, very little settled, and with trails going in all directions. My sailing orders were "steer south, and keep to the best beaten track," and it seemed like embarking on the ocean without a compass. The rolling brown waves on which you see a horse a mile and a half off impress one strangely, and at noon the sky darkened up for another storm, the mountains swept down in blackness to the Plains, and the higher peaks took on a ghastly grimness horrid to behold. It was first very cold, then very hot, and finally settled down to a fierce east-windy cold, difficult to endure. It was free and breezy, however, and my horse was companionable. Sometimes herds of cattle were browsing on the sun-cured grass, then herds of horses. Occasionally I met a horseman with a rifle lying across his saddle, or a wagon of the ordinary sort, but oftener I saw a wagon with a white tilt, of the kind known as a "Prairie Schooner," laboring across the grass, or a train of them, accompanied by herds, mules, and horsemen, bearing emigrants and their household goods in dreary exodus from the Western States to the much-vaunted prairies of Colorado.

The host and hostess of one of these wagons invited me to join their mid-day meal, I providing tea (which they had not tasted for four weeks) and they hominy. They had been three months on the journey from Illinois, and their oxen were so lean and weak that they expected to be another month in reaching Wet Mountain Valley. They had buried a child *en route*, had lost several oxen, and were rather out of heart. Owing to their long isolation and the monotony of the march they had lost count of events, and seemed like people of another planet. They wanted me to join them, but their rate of travel was too slow, so we parted with mutual expressions of good will, and as their white tilt went "hull down" in the distance on the lonely prairie sea, I felt sadder than I often feel on taking leave of old acquaintances. That night they must have been nearly frozen, camping out in the deep snow in the fierce wind. I met afterwards 2,000 lean Texan cattle, herded by three wild-looking men on horseback, followed by two wagons containing women, children, and rifles. They had traveled 1,000 miles. Then I saw two prairie wolves, like jackals, with gray fur, cowardly creatures, which fled from me with long leaps.

The windy cold became intense, and for the next eleven miles I rode a race with the coming storm. At the top of every prairie roll I expected to see Denver, but it was not till nearly five that from a considerable height I looked down upon the great "City of the Plains," the metropolis of the Territories. There the great braggart city lay spread out, brown and treeless, upon the brown and treeless plain, which seemed to nourish nothing but wormwood and the Spanish bayonet. The shallow Platte, shriveled into a narrow stream with a shingly bed six times too large for it, and fringed by shriveled cotton-wood, wound along by Denver, and two miles up its course I saw a great sand-storm, which in a few minutes covered the city, blotting it out with a dense brown cloud. Then with gusts of wind the snow-storm began, and I had to trust entirely to Birdie's sagacity for finding Evans's shantie. She had been there once before only, but carried me direct to it over rough ground and trenches. Gleefully Mrs. Evans and the children ran out to welcome the pet pony, and I was received most hospitably, and made warm and comfortable, though the house consists only of a kitchen and two bed closets. My budget of news from "the park" had to be brought out constantly, and I wondered how much I had to tell. It was past eleven when we breakfasted the next morning. It was cloudless with an intense frost, and six inches of snow on the ground, and everybody thought it too cold to get up and light the fire. I had intended to leave Birdie at Denver, but Governor Hunt and Mr. Byers of the *Rocky Mountain News* both advised me to travel on horseback rather than by train and stage telling me that I should be quite safe, and Governor Hunt drew out a route for me and gave me a circular letter to the settlers along it.

Denver is no longer the Denver of Hepworth Dixon. A shooting affray in the street is as rare as in Liverpool, and one no longer sees men dangling to the lamp-posts when one looks out in the morning! It is a busy place, the *entrepôt* and distributing point for an immense district, with good shops, some factories, fair hotels, and the usual deformities and refinements of civilization. Peltry shops abound, and sportsman, hunter, miner, teamster, emigrant, can be completely rigged out at fifty different stores. At Denver, people who come from the East to try the "camp cure" now so fashionable, get their outfit of wagon, driver, horses, tent, bedding, and stove, and start for the mountains. Asthmatic people are there in such numbers as to warrant the holding of an "asthmatic convention" of patients cured and benefited. Numbers of invalids who cannot bear the rough life of the mountains fill its hotels and boarding-houses, and others who have been partially restored by a summer of camping out, go into the city in the winter to complete the cure. It stands at a height of 5,000 feet, on an enormous plain, and has a most glorious view of the Rocky Range. I should hate even to spend a week there. The sight of those glories so near and yet out of reach would make me nearly crazy. Denver is at present the terminus of the Kansas Pacific Railroad. It has a line connecting it with the Union Pacific Railroad at Cheyenne, and by means of the Denver and Rio Grande Railroad, open for about 200 miles, it is expecting to reach into Mexico. It has also had the enterprise, by means of another narrow-gauge railroad, to push its way right up into the mining districts near Gray's Peak. The number of "saloons" in the streets impresses one, and everywhere one meets the characteristic loafers of a frontier town, who find it hard even for a few days or hours to submit to the restraints of civilization, as hard as I did to ride sidewise to Governor Hunt's office. To Denver men go to spend the savings of months of hard work in the maddest dissipation, and there are such characters as "Comanche Bill," "Buffalo Bill," "Wild Bill," and "Mountain Jim," go on the spree, and find the kind of notoriety they seek.

A large number of Indians added to the harlequin appearance of the Denver streets the day I was there. They belonged to the Ute tribe, through which I had to pass, and Governor Hunt introduced me to a fine-looking young chief, very well dressed in beaded hide, and bespoke his courtesy for me if I needed it. The Indian stores and fur stores and fur depôts interested me most. The crowds in the streets, perhaps owing to the snow on the ground, were almost solely masculine. I only saw five women the whole day. There were men in every rig:

hunters and trappers in buckskin clothing; men of the Plains with belts and revolvers, in great blue cloaks, relics of the war; teamsters in leathern suits; horsemen in fur coats and caps and buffalo-hide boots with the hair outside, and camping blankets behind their huge Mexican saddles; Broadway dandies in light kid gloves; rich English sporting tourists, clean, comely, and supercilious looking; and hundreds of Indians on their small ponies, the men wearing buckskin suits sewn with beads, and red blankets, with faces painted vermilion and hair hanging lank and straight, and squaws much bundled up, riding astride with furs over their saddles.

Town tired and confused me, and in spite of Mrs. Evans's kind hospitality, I was glad when a man brought Birdie at nine yesterday morning. He said she was a little demon, she had done nothing but buck, and had bucked him off on the bridge! I found that he had put a curb on her, and whenever she dislikes anything she resents it by bucking. I rode sidewise till I was well through the town, long enough to produce a severe pain in my spine, which was not relieved for some time even after I had changed my position. It was a lovely Indian summer day, so warm that the snow on the ground looked an incongruity. I rode over the Plains for some time, then gradually reached the rolling country along the base of the mountains, and a stream with cotton-woods along it, and settlers' houses about every half-mile. I passed and met wagons frequently, and picked up a muff containing a purse with 500 dollars in it, which I afterwards had the great pleasure of restoring to the owner. Several times I crossed the narrow track of the quaint little Rio Grande Railroad, so that it was a very cheerful ride.

RANCH, PLUM CREEK, *October 24.*

You must understand that in Colorado travel, unless on the main road and in the larger settlements, there are neither hotels nor taverns, and that it is the custom for the settlers to receive travelers, charging them at the usual hotel rate for accommodation. It is a very satisfactory arrangement. However, at Ranch, my first halting place, the host was unwilling to receive people in this way, I afterwards found, or I certainly should not have presented my credentials at the door of a large frame house, with large barns and a generally prosperous look. The host, who opened the door, looked repellant, but his wife, a very agreeable, lady-like-looking woman, said they could give me a bed on a sofa. The house was the most pretentious I have yet seen, being papered and carpeted, and there were two "hired girls." There was a lady there from Laramie, who kindly offered to receive me into her room, a very tall, elegant person, remarkable as being the first woman who had settled in the Rocky Mountains. She had been trying the "camp cure" for three months, and was then on her way home. She had a wagon with beds, tent, tent floor, cooking-stove, and every camp luxury, a light buggy, a man to manage everything, and a most superior "hired girl." She was consumptive and frail in strength, but a very attractive person, and her stories of the perils and limitations of her early life at Fort Laramie were very interesting. Still I "wearied," as I had arrived early in the afternoon, and could not out of politeness retire and write to you. At meals the three "hired men" and two "hired girls" eat with the family. I soon found that there was a screw loose in the house, and was glad to leave early the next morning, although it was obvious that a storm was coming on.

I saw the toy car of the Rio Grande Railroad whirl past, all cushioned and warm, and rather wished I were in it, and not out among the snow on the bleak hill side. I only got on four miles when the storm came on so badly that I got into a kitchen where eleven wretched travelers were taking shelter, with the snow melting on them and dripping on the floor. I had learned the art of "being agreeable" so well at the Chalmers's, and practised it so successfully during the two hours I was there, by paring potatoes and making scones, that when I left, though the hosts kept "an accommodation house for travelers," they would take nothing for my entertainment, because they said I was such "good company"! The storm moderated a little, and at one I saddled Birdie, and rode four more miles, crossing a frozen creek, the ice of which broke and let the pony through, to her great alarm. I cannot describe my feelings on this ride, produced by the utter loneliness, the silence and dumbness of all things, the snow falling quietly without wind, the obliterated mountains, the darkness, the intense cold, and the unusual and appalling aspect of nature. All life was in a shroud, all work and travel suspended. There was not a foot-mark or wheel-mark. There was nothing to be afraid of; and though I can't exactly say that I enjoyed the ride, yet there was the pleasant feeling of gaining health every hour.

When the snow darkness began to deepen towards evening, the track became quite illegible, and when I found myself at this romantically situated cabin, I was thankful to find that they could give me shelter. The scene was a solemn one, and reminded me of a description in Whittier's *Snow-Bound*. All the stock came round the cabin with mute appeals for shelter. Sheep dogs got in, and would not be kicked out. Men went out muffled up, and came back shivering and shaking the snow from their feet. The churn was put by the stove. Later on, a most pleasant settler, on his way to Denver, came in his wagon having been snow blocked two miles off, where he had been obliged to leave it and bring his horses on here. The "Grey Mare" had a stentorian voice, smoked a clay pipe which she passed to her children, raged at English people, derided the courtesy of English manners, and considered that "Please," "Thank you," and the like, were "all bosh" when life was so short and busy. And still the snow fell softly, and the air and earth were silent.

Letter X

*

✦✿✦✿✦✿✦✿✦✿✦✿✦✿✦✿✦✿✦✿✦✿✦✿✦✿✦✿✦

A WHITE WORLD—BAD TRAVELING—A MILLIONAIRE'S
HOME—PLEASANT PARK—PERRY'S PARK—STOCK-RAIS-
ING—A CATTLE KING—THE ARKANSAS DIVIDE—BIRDIE'S
SAGACITY—LUXURY—MONUMENT PARK—DEFERENCE TO
PREJUDICE—A DEATH SCENE—THE MANITOU—A LOOSE
SHOE—THE UTE PASS—BERGENS PARK—A SETTLER'S
HOME—HAYDEN'S DIVIDE—SHARP CRITICISM—SPEAK-
ING THE TRUTH.

✦✿✦✿✦✿✦✿✦✿✦✿✦✿✦✿✦✿✦✿✦✿✦✿✦✿✦✿✦

COLORADO SPRINGS, *October 28.*

It is difficult to make this anything of a letter. I have been
riding for a whole week, seeing wonders and greatly enjoying the singular adventurousness and novelty of my
tour, but ten hours or more daily spent in the saddle in
this rarefied, intoxicating air, disposes one to sleep rather
than to write in the evening, and is far from conducive to
mental brilliancy. The observing faculties are developed,
and the reflective lie dormant.

That night on which I last wrote was the coldest I have
yet felt. I pulled the rag carpet from the floor and covered
myself with it, but could not get warm. The sun rose
gloriously on a shrouded earth. Barns, road, shrubs, fences,
river, lake, all lay under the glittering snow. It was light
and powdery, and sparkled like diamonds. Not a breath
of wind stirred, there was not a sound. I had to wait till a
passing horseman had broken the track, but soon after I